DEPARTMENT OF ENGLISH LOCAL HISTORY

OCCASIONAL PAPERS

Second Series Number 3

The Hidation of Northamptonshire

by

CYRIL HART

LEICESTER UNIVERSITY PRESS

DEPARTMENT OF ENGLISH LOCAL HISTORY

OCCASIONAL PAPERS

Second Series

EDITED BY ALAN EVERITT

Number 3

The Hidation of Northamptonshire

by

CYRIL HART

M.A., M.B., F.R.Hist.S.

LEICESTER UNIVERSITY PRESS

1970

First published in 1970 by
Leicester University Press

Distributed in North America by
Humanities Press Inc., New York

Set in Monotype Baskerville
Printed in Great Britain at
The Broadwater Press, Welwyn Garden City, Hertfordshire

SBN 7185 2021 1

This volume is published with
the help of a grant from the late
Miss Isobel Thornley's Bequest
to the University of London

To

R. WELLDON FINN

in appreciation of his

Domesday studies

CONTENTS

LIST OF ABBREVIATIONS	page 7
PREFACE	8
INTRODUCTION	9
THE INITIAL HIDATION	11
THE ORIGIN OF NORTHAMPTONSHIRE	12
THE COUNTY HIDAGE	15
THE NORTHAMPTONSHIRE GELD ROLL	16
THE POST-CONQUEST HIDATION OF INDIVIDUAL ESTATES	21
THE HIDE AND THE PLOUGHLAND	24
THE PLOUGHLANDS: A NEW HYPOTHESIS	28
THE PLOUGHLAND ASSESSMENT OF CROWN HOLDINGS	28
THE PRE-CONQUEST HIDATION OF INDIVIDUAL ESTATES	32
THE BADBY CHARTER	35
HIDATION AT DIFFERENT PERIODS	37
THE CHANGING PATTERN OF HIDATION	39
THE DANISH INFLUENCE ON HIDATION	43
THE COUNTY HIDAGE—A POSTSCRIPT	45
APPENDIX: THE HUNDREDAL ASSESSMENTS OF THE NORTHAMPTONSHIRE DOMESDAY	47

LIST OF ABBREVIATIONS

a.	acre.
ASC.	Anglo-Saxon Chronicle.
bov.	bovate.
CS.	*Cartularium Saxonicum*, ed. W. de G. Birch, 3 vols., 1885–93; charters quoted by number.
Chron. Rams.	*Chronicon Abbatiae Rameseiensis*, ed. W. Dunn Macray, Rolls Series, 1886.
DB.	Domesday Book.
EHD.	*English Historical Documents*, vol. 1, ed. D. Whitelock, 1955.
EHR.	*English Historical Review*.
h.	hide.
K.	Kemble, J. M. (ed.), *Codex Diplomaticus Ævi Saxonici*, 6 vols., 1839–48; charters quoted by number.
p.	ploughland.
PN.	(followed by name of county) volume in the series produced by the English Place-Name Society.
R.	Robertson, A. J. (ed.), *Anglo-Saxon Charters*, 2nd edn, 1956.
TRE.	In the time of King Edward the Confessor.
v.	virgate.
VCH.	(followed by name of county) volume in the Victoria County History series.

PREFACE

SOME apology is called for regarding this paper, which is but one of a series I have prepared concerning the early assessment of the Danelaw shires for taxation and other public burdens. That for Huntingdonshire has appeared already; Cambridgeshire, Bedfordshire, and Nottinghamshire are completed and awaiting publication, and work is proceeding on the remainder. From these studies a general theory of the pattern of assessment has emerged. The evidence recorded for one shire supports that of another; the whole thing interlocks, and there are difficulties in presenting the material for any one shire in isolation. Nevertheless, each shire does have its own unique features, and for the establishment of the general theory the evidence of each shire must be displayed in detail. Eventually I hope to bring together the results of all this work in a more comprehensive statement; meanwhile, the indulgence of readers is requested, when allusions are made to the general theory without full reference to the supporting evidence from other shires.

My best thanks are due to the Trustees of the Isobel Thornley Bequest for a grant towards publication, and to R. Welldon Finn for his generous and painstaking work checking the tables in the Appendix.

CYRIL HART

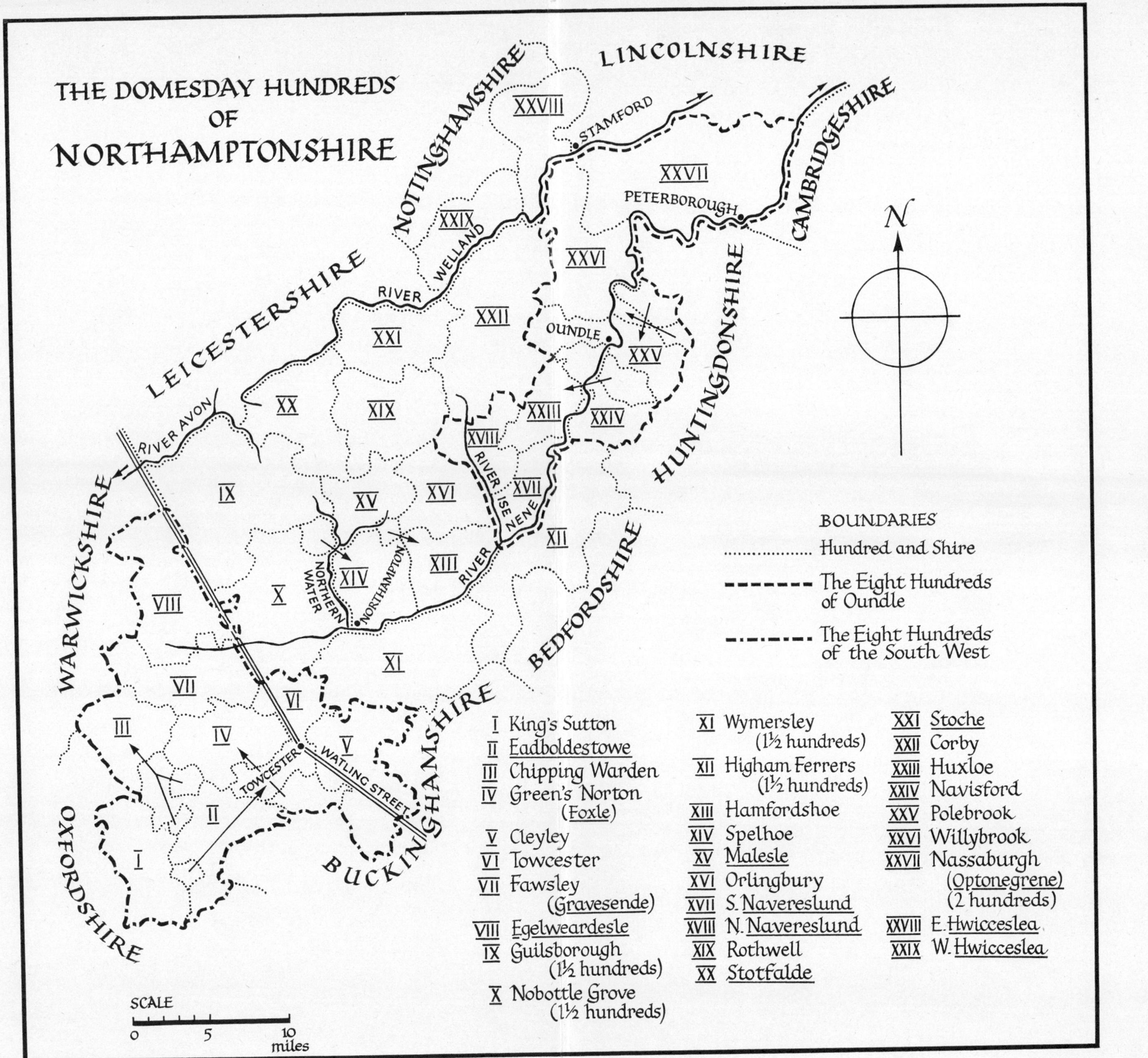

NOTE: *Hundred names that did not survive the Norman Period are underlined.*

INTRODUCTION

THE origin of the English hide is lost in the mists of antiquity. The earliest charters, the earliest codes of laws (apart from those of the Kentish kings), the earliest narrative sources of the Anglo-Saxon period, all speak of hides as of a long-established institution. It is very probable that from the outset the hide was a unit of assessment imposed by the king through the agency of his ministers, for purposes of taxation and for the organization of military service and other forms of obligation falling on the landholders. In the eighth century in Mercia, each tribal unit was assessed at a round number of hides, and we can be sure from the charter evidence that this sum was broken up among the individual holdings of members of the tribe, in rough proportion to the values of their estates.

The territory which became Northamptonshire was part of Mercia at this period, but little evidence has survived of the pattern of tribal settlement within the area, and we know hardly anything of the initial hidation of any of its individual estate holdings. The Scandinavian occupation of the late ninth century obliterated all records of this first hidation, and we can only speculate to what extent—if at all—the fresh system of assessment imposed upon the territory some forty or fifty years later followed the original pre-Scandinavian pattern.

It is this second hidation which chiefly concerns us here. The Northamptonshire assessment presents several unique features, and we are fortunate in that the materials recording it are richer than for any other county. They have attracted the attention of a succession of distinguished scholars, and it would be wrong to embark upon a fresh interpretation without first bringing to notice the major contributions of those who have gone over the ground before.

The modern study of Northamptonshire's hidation commenced with the late J. Horace Round's epoch-making analysis of the Northamptonshire Geld Roll, which was published in 1895.[1] Dating as it does from within ten years of the Norman Conquest, the Geld Roll is our earliest surviving fiscal record for an English county, and incidentally, for any unit of local government in the whole of medieval Europe. Moreover, it supplies information about conditions obtaining in the time of Edward the Confessor, and because of this it is a key document for our understanding of the origin and early history of the shire. Its significance was further illustrated by F. W. Maitland in 1897, when he used Round's analysis to demonstrate the connection between the 32 hundreds

[1] J. H. Round, *Feudal England*, 1895, pp. 58–9, 147–56.

recorded in the Geld Roll, and the 3,200 hides for which Northamptonshire was assessed in the County Hidage, a document originating certainly no later than the first decade of the eleventh century.[1]

By the time of Maitland's discovery, Round had commenced his work upon the Northamptonshire Domesday. He summarized his initial findings in a characteristic paper in 1900,[2] following it up two years later with a full-scale introduction and translation of the Northamptonshire section of Domesday Book.[3] At the same time, he translated and published the Northamptonshire Survey, which records the hidage of the county hundred by hundred some forty years after Domesday.[4] Already, in 1898, F. Baring had been working on the Northamptonshire Survey, and his conclusions can be studied in two more papers on the hidation of Northamptonshire, which also appeared in 1902.[5]

Baring's papers marked the end of this great burst of activity, and only comparatively minor and incidental contributions to our knowledge of the county's hidation have appeared since. The first of these was the English Place-Name Society's volume on the county, published in 1933.[6] Besides facilitating the identification of Domesday holdings, this book contains helpful maps and a useful introduction. In 1939, Miss A. J. Robertson produced a new edition and translation of the Northamptonshire Geld Roll, which enables several corrections to be made to Round's pioneer analysis.[7] R. H. Hoyt discussed the hidation of the Crown estates in 1950, but his methods and conclusions are open to criticism.[8] Finally, H. C. Darby's *Domesday Geography of Midland England*, which appeared in 1954, supplies another useful series of maps, summarizing the main geographical factors influencing local topography at the time of the Domesday Inquest.

Both Round and Maitland appreciated that full value could not be extracted from the surviving information until the hidage assessments of individual estates recorded in the Domesday Survey had been reconstructed hundred by hundred for the whole county. The process is a long and arduous one, beset with many difficulties of identification and analysis. The result of it all is now made available as an Appendix to this paper. These reconstructed hundredal statistics form the starting point for a fresh approach to the hidation of the shire.

[1] F. W. Maitland, *Domesday Book and Beyond*, 1897, 2nd edn (Fontana) 1960, pp. 525–7.
[2] J. H. Round, 'The Hidation of Northamptonshire', *EHR*, xv, 1900, pp. 78–86.
[3] *VCH, Northants.*, I, 1902, pp. 257–356. [4] *Ibid.*, pp. 357–89.
[5] F. Baring, 'The Hidation of Northamptonshire in 1086', *EHR*, XVII, 1902, pp. 76–83, 470–9.
[6] J. E. B. Gover, A. Mawer, and F. M. Stenton, *PN Northants.*, 1933.
[7] A. J. Robertson, *Anglo-Saxon Charters*, 1939, pp. 230–7, 481–4.
[8] R. H. Hoyt, *The Royal Demesne in English Constitutional History: 1066-1272*, 1950, pp. 36–51, 59–63.

THE INITIAL HIDATION

It is desirable to preface the detailed study of Northamptonshire's assessment in the tenth and eleventh centuries with a brief account of the area's initial hidation. For this purpose, our definition of the hide as a unit of assessment "imposed by the King . . . upon holdings of land" requires qualification; for the east Midlands, including most if not all of the territory which became Northamptonshire, was settled in the fifth century by members of a loose confederation of tribes known collectively as the Middle Angles, and there is no evidence that this confederation was ever ruled by a dynasty of its own. Its hidage could well have been imposed in the first instance by some overlord, or *bretwalda* to use the Anglo-Saxon term, who was in a position to raise tribute from all the tribes and kingdoms of the Anglo-Saxon settlement.

This is not the place to argue the date at which such an assessment could have been made; conceivably Edwin, the first Northumbrian *bretwalda*, was the initiator. He was active in the third decade of the seventh century. Once the hidation was established, one assumes that successive *bretwaldas* inherited the individual tribal assessments from their predecessors; no doubt modifications were introduced to allow for extension of the area under settlement and to meet variations in the fortunes of particular communities, but it is neither reasonable nor necessary to suppose that the general pattern of hidation underwent revolutionary changes with every change of overlord. No doubt the principle of continuity was as powerful a factor here as with other aspects of early English society.

Whatever the date of its original imposition, the pages of Bede establish that the whole of England, except the extreme south-west, was hidated by the time of the seventh-century Northumbrian *bretwaldas*. A century later, when the bretwaldaship had passed into the hands of the Mercian kings, each kingdom or tribal unit under their jurisdiction was assessed at a round number of hides. A document called the Tribal Hidage[1] lists these assessments, but unfortunately, several of the communities listed therein remain unlocated. Those which may have occupied part of the later county of Northampton include the *North Gyrwa*, a people of 600 hides who lived in the fenland to the north of the River Nene,[2] the *Widerigga*, also of 600 hides centred probably between Wittering and Werrington,[3] and the *Herefinna*, of 1,200 hides, settled in the territory which became the south part of Huntingdonshire and south-eastern Northamptonshire.[4] Most of the remainder of what was to become Northamptonshire was settled by Middle Anglian peoples.

[1] Best edited by W. de Gray Birch, *CS* 297. I hope to discuss this in detail in a future paper.

[2] *VCH, Northants.*, I, pp. 250–1; *The Chronicle of Hugh Candidus*, ed. W. T. Mellows, 1949, p. 4.

[3] *PN Northants.*, p. xiv.

[4] A. Mawer and F. M. Stenton, *The Place-Names of Bedfordshire and Huntingdonshire*, 1926, pp. xviii–xix.

Whether or not these suggested identifications gain general acceptance, we may be quite sure that in the eighth century the whole of the large tract of territory which later became Northamptonshire was occupied by one or more of the peoples listed in the Tribal Hidage, and from charter evidence we may deduce further that here as elsewhere in England the overall assessment of each tribal unit was distributed among the individual holdings of its members, according to the value of their estates. The whole area remained subject to Mercia, and the initial hidation survived intact, until the Scandinavian settlement of A.D. 877. There followed a brief interregnum, under Danish earls, until the re-conquest of the territory by the English Crown, with the consequent formation of the modern county.

THE ORIGIN OF NORTHAMPTONSHIRE

The events leading to the formation of the county of Northampton are recorded in a long annal entered under the year 920 (*recte* 917) in the Parker Chronicle. We are told that before Easter that year, King Edward the Elder ordered the borough of Towcester to be occupied and built. The following July, the Danish armies from Northampton and Leicester joined to make an unsuccessful attack on the newly fortified borough. In the autumn, King Edward established himself with his army at Passenham, while Towcester was provided with a stone wall. This led to the surrender of the Danish Earl Thurferth, with all his armed retainers, together with all the army which belonged to Northampton, as far north as the River Welland.

We learn from this account two things: first that Watling Street, which had been established as the boundary between English and Danish government by King Alfred's peace with Guthrum in 886–90, was still the frontier in 917.[1] Second, the Danish army of Northampton was drawn from a territory which had the River Welland for its northern boundary. The summer after the events which have been related above, King Edward consolidated his victory by moving north and occupying Stamford; thereafter the Danish army settlers, having lost their autonomy, never again governed for themselves the territory of Northamptonshire.

To digress for a moment, Passenham and Towcester remained as royal estates until after the Norman Conquest.[2] The latter borough gave its name to

[1] *EHD*, I, pp. 380–1.

[2] Towcester and Passenham lie just to the south-west of Watling Street, and between them was the royal *burh* of Whittlebury, from which King Athelstan issued a code of laws in *c.* 940. All three *burhs* lay in Whittlewood Forest. Danish-occupied Northampton lay a few miles to the north-east. See further F. M. Stenton in *PN Northants.*, pp. xix, xxi.

one of the hundreds of Northamptonshire, and of the remaining seven hundreds lying partly or wholly to the south-west of Watling Street, three more were likewise named after royal manors at the time of Domesday.[1] As to the significance of this, Professor Cam's researches have served to reinforce the opinion first put forward by Sir Frank Stenton, that "in the tenth century, local divisions regarded each as a hundred hides were being annexed to royal estates."[2] This point is mentioned here, because (as will be shown) the hidation of the eight Northamptonshire hundreds lying to the south-west of Watling Street presents features which indicate that they were dealt with as a unit, and it is quite likely that this identity derives from conditions obtaining there before the rest of what became Northamptonshire was re-conquered from the Danes by Edward the Elder.

We do not know much about the form of government imposed upon the surrounding territory by the Danish host centred on Northampton after the settlement of 877, but we have a good idea of the limits of its jurisdiction. As we have seen, the Parker Chronicle gives the River Welland as its northern boundary, and implies that Watling Street limited it to the south-west. Eastwards, its bounds marched with those of the army centred on Huntingdon. It seems very likely, therefore, that for the most part the outer limits of jurisdiction were coterminous with the bounds of that part of Northamptonshire lying to the north-east of Watling Street. When Edward the Elder gained control of this area, he had only to add to it the eight hundreds to the south-west of Watling Street, and two more hundreds lying near Stamford on the north bank of the Welland,[3] to create the full-sized county as we know it in Domesday Book.

This assertion immediately leads us into deep waters, for nowhere in the history books do we find Edward the Elder portrayed as the architect of the east Midland shires.[4] Northamptonshire, Huntingdonshire, Bedfordshire, and

[1] Sutton, Norton, and Fawsley. Only three of the 24 hundreds north-east of Watling Street were named after royal manors, and these formed a compact group (Rothwell, *Stoche*, and Corby) in which lay the royal forest of Rockingham. H. M. Cam, 'Manerium cum Hundredo', in *Liberties and Communities in Medieval England*, 2nd edn, 1963, pp. 64–90, especially p. 82, n. 9.

[2] Cam, *op. cit.*, pp. 84–5; F. M. Stenton, *The Early History of the Abbey of Abingdon*, 1913, p. 47.

[3] East and West *Hwicceslea*. Probably the territory of these two hundreds had been administered until this time by the Danish host centred on Stamford. Their inclusion within Northamptonshire by Edward the Elder seems to have been dictated by the necessity of bringing the hidation of that shire up to 3,200, to fit it within the duodecimal pattern shown by the rest of the shires of the County Hidage (see Table I). The explanation of Stamford's isolation from the administrative units to the south and west which was offered by H. M. Chadwick (*Studies in Anglo-Saxon Institutions*, 1905, pp. 209–10) and tentatively accepted by H. R. Loyn in *The Making of Stamford*, ed. Alan Rogers, 1965, p. 30, cannot be sustained, for it rests on the false assumption that Northamptonshire was allotted 30 hundreds (actually 32) and Huntingdonshire 4 (actually 4 *double* hundreds = 8).

[4] The nearest approach to such a claim that I can find is contained in D. Whitelock's *The Beginnings of English Society*, 1952, p. 79: "Our shires of the East and North Midlands and of York have developed

Cambridgeshire appear together as a compact group in the County Hidage, but Liebermann suggested as a date for that document the early years of the eleventh century, and C. S. Taylor, in an ably constructed paper, argued that the Mercian shires originated at about the same period—in other words, that the County Hidage was recording an organization which had only just been brought into being.[1] Professor Finberg's important recent study of the rubrication of Hemming's Cartulary[2] appears at first sight to support Taylor's conclusions, but the evidence cited both by Taylor and by Finberg, reduced to its essentials, shows just this: in or about the year 1007, the Midland territories dependent upon towns commenced to be described as shires, as had long been the case in Wessex. Some time within the next ten years, the shire of Winchcombe was amalgamated (possibly one should say reunited) with Gloucestershire; but with this sole exception, I can find no evidence to indicate that this change in terminology, this specific application of the word 'shire', coincided with a reorganization of local government in the territories concerned.

Indeed, my own studies on hidage lead me to believe that this was not the case. I believe that the east and north Midland counties as we know them were created and hidated soon after their conquest by King Edward the Elder and his sister Æthelflæd,[3] and that the County Hidage, therefore, whatever its date as a document, describes an administrative situation which had remained unchanged since the second or third decade of the tenth century.[4]

---

from the areas attached to Danish boroughs after the Viking settlement, while the shires of the South West Midlands, which are similarly named from a single borough, probably owe their origin to a tenth-century reorganisation which may have taken the West Saxon shires as its model." F. M. Stenton, in *PN Northants.*, p. xviii, states: "the county of medieval and modern times represents the district occupied by a particular Danish *here* late in the ninth century." W. J. Corbett, in *Cambridge Medieval History*, III, 1922, pp. 366–7, ascribes the creation of the county hidation to King Athelstan, but supplies no evidence. H. R. Loyn, *op. cit.*, p. 27, says: "the permanent shiring of the eastern Midlands was effected ... presumably during the latter part of the tenth century."

[1] *Transactions of the Bristol and Gloucestershire Archaeological Society*, XXI, 1898, pp. 32–57; XXXII, pp. 109–39; re-edited by H. P. R. Finberg in *Gloucestershire Studies*, 1957, pp. 17–45.

[2] H. P. R. Finberg, *The Early Charters of the West Midlands*, 1961, pp. 15–18, 228–35.

[3] See F. T. Wainwright, 'Æthelflæd, Lady of the Mercians', in *The Anglo-Saxons*, ed. P. Clemoes, 1959, pp. 53–69.

[4] C. F. Slade expresses a similar opinion in relation to Staffordshire: "The hidation ... can be traced ... certainly to the end and probably to the middle of the tenth century."—*VCH, Staffs.*, IV, 1958, p. 5. In a recent paper on Huntingdonshire, I gave charter evidence to show that its hidation was established by 937 at the latest. See *Proceedings of the Cambridge Antiquarian Society*, LXI, 1968, p. 58.

THE COUNTY HIDAGE

Reference has been made already to the County Hidage, a list of shires and their hidages surviving in four versions, first collated and discussed by Maitland in 1897. The list may be summarized as follows:

Table I: The County Hidage compared with Domesday Hidage

Information from the County Hidage		*Number of Domesday Hundreds*	*Domesday Hidage*
Shire	*Hidage*		
Wiltshire	4,800	40	4,050
Bedfordshire	1,200	12	1,214*
Cambridgeshire	2,500	16	1,220*
Huntingdonshire	850	4 (double)	828*
Northamptonshire	3,200	32	1,244*
Gloucestershire	2,400	39	2,388
Worcestershire	1,200	12	1,204†
Herefordshire	1,500	19	1,324
Warwickshire	1,200	12	1,338
Oxfordshire	2,400	22	2,412
Shropshire	2,400	13	1,245
Cheshire	1,200	12	512
Staffordshire	500	5	513‡

*My own figures. †C. S. Taylor in *Gloucestershire Studies*, p. 42.
‡Slade in *VCH, Staffs.*, IV, p. 2.

The order of counties in the above list is the same as that in which they appear in the original documents, but reference to a map will show that the list groups the counties silently on a topographical basis, which I have illustrated in the table by spaces between the groupings. Wiltshire's position at the top of the list is clearly anomalous; it is the only West Saxon shire to be included. The rest comprise all those Mercian shires which were hidated at the time of Domesday. The four counties of Derby, Nottingham, Leicester, and Lincoln, which were dependent on the Five Boroughs, and carucated at the time of Domesday, are omitted from the County Hidage; so too are Yorkshire, Lancashire, and East Anglia, none of which was hidated in Domesday Book. Indeed, the County

Hidage forms our earliest record of the line of cleavage between the hidated and the carucated shires.

The group which concerns us most closely here is the one comprising the four east Midland counties of Bedfordshire, Cambridgeshire, Huntingdonshire, and Northamptonshire. As with other groupings in the County Hidage, this association is not purely fortuitous, for these counties share a common administrative history. They were re-conquered by Edward the Elder in a single series of campaigns; at the time of the Norman Conquest they formed a single earldom; and although they were not all included within a single Domesday circuit, when Domesday Book was compiled the circuit returns for the individual counties were rearranged so that these four east Midland shires appear as consecutive entries.

Within this grouping we may make an immediate subdivision, for whereas the Domesday hidages of Huntingdonshire and Bedfordshire approximate very closely to their County Hidage assessments, we find in the cases of Cambridgeshire and Northamptonshire that this is not so; there has been a reduction of 50 per cent in the former shire and 60 per cent in the latter, between the time of the County Hidage and Domesday. It is this reduction which invests the study of Northamptonshire's hidation with much of its interest. Before we can discuss this in detail, however, we must first deal with the county's Geld Roll.

THE NORTHAMPTONSHIRE GELD ROLL

This is the name customarily given to a document which survives only in a twelfth-century version entered in the Peterborough *Liber Niger*. It is improbable that the original record took the form of a roll, but its traditional title is by now too firmly rooted for it to be changed for a more accurate description, such as the Northamptonshire Geld Inquest. Various considerations, detailed below, combine to suggest that it was compiled by an Englishman to account for the poor and uneven yield from the county of a geld levied within a decade of the Norman Conquest. The geld itself is never referred to in terms of money, a fact which together with its use of the vernacular distinguishes the document sharply from the geld accounts of the south-western shires compiled at the time of Domesday. If we accept the claim put forward by Professor Galbraith that the collection of the geld, which had been discontinued by Edward the Confessor in 1051 and re-introduced immediately after the Conquest, very quickly became an annual affair, then we may well conclude that the Northamptonshire record dates from very early in the Conqueror's reign.[1]

[1] V. H. Galbraith, *The Making of Domesday Book*, 1961, pp. 97–8. I think it fair to say that Professor

The document concerns itself fundamentally with the hidage assessment of the shire, rather than the geld raised from it. We do not even know at what rate the geld was levied in that particular year, and it is unsafe to assume from this silence that the rate was the normal one of two shillings per hide. Each hundred is described in turn. First, the current hidage assigned to the hundred is compared with its assessment TRE (*'swa hit was on Eadwardes dege kynges'*). In every case, the total hidage is the same for both periods. Then the number of hides within the hundred which have actually rendered geld (*'gewered'*) is given. Next appears a figure for the *'inland'* of the hundred, which was exempt from the geld. When the particular hundred happens to contain individual estates which for some reason or other are totally exempt from the geld, this is then referred to and their hidage given. Finally, the account allots a figure for the hidage of the 'waste' of each hundred. The figure for waste is clearly arrived at by totting up the hidage figures for the land which gelded, the *inland*, and the exempt estates, and subtracting the result from the total hidage currently allotted to the hundred.

The word *inland* in the present context means 'land exempt from the geld', and in the later geld accounts for the south-western shires it can clearly be equated with the demesne of the baronial estates within each hundred. The baronial demesne was hidated, but it did not pay geld at the time of Domesday. But in the case of the Northamptonshire Geld Roll, the hidage figures for *inland* allotted to the hundreds of the south-western half of the county are much higher than those for the north-eastern half; moreover they are given in round numbers too consistently for this to be due to chance; they suggest therefore an arbitrary and unrealistically high assessment, hundred by hundred. This is not the case in the north-eastern end of the county, for which the figures appear to have been obtained by adding up the *inland* hidage assessment of the individual baronial estates within each hundred. These differences between the *inland* assessments for the two halves of the shire are best illustrated by listing the *inland* hidage figures hundred by hundred in topographical order, thus:

17½ south-western hundreds (map nos. I–XI; XIII–XV; XIX and XX): 40, 45, 40, 30, 40, 40, 35, 40, (68 + 72),[1] 60, 25,[2] 25, 30, 20, 40.

Average = 37 hides *inland* per hundred.

Galbraith's claim, that the geld was raised annually after the Conquest, is now generally accepted by historians of the period.

[1] The two 'hundred-and-a-half' units of Nobottle Grove and Guilsborough had a total *inland* assessment of 140 hides.

[2] For Spelhoe hundred we have the interesting statement in the Geld Roll that 25 hides are 'borough land', and exempt from the geld. These are included in the total assessment of the hundred, and Round suggested (*Feudal England*, p. 156) that they represent the geld liability of the borough of Northampton. It is noteworthy that Spelhoe is the only hundred for which no entry for *inland* is given in the Geld Roll,

14½ north-eastern hundreds (map nos. XII; XVI–XVIII; XXI–XXIX): 44, 24½, 59, 10½, 11½, 15, 14, 20, 11, 27, 34, 40.

Average = 21½ hides *inland* per hundred.

We have here one of the cruces of the county's hidation, for our ability to understand fully the Northamptonshire Geld Roll hinges on this problem of the *inland* and its assessment. The late J. H. Round, who had a remarkable flair for arriving at radical solutions to this type of puzzle, put forward the hypothesis that these figures for *inland* represent in fact a stage in the reduction of the hidation imposed upon the shire.[1] This solution is undoubtedly too simple, for it does not take into account the differences in assessment between the two groups of hundreds enumerated above, differences of which Round was not aware. Furthermore, there is ample evidence from other shires whose hidages were not reduced during this period, that the exemption of *inland* from the geld was a general concession throughout the country, and not confined to Northamptonshire. Such exemption did not, however, cause the *inland* to lose its hidation; except in the case of the Crown estates, the *inland* usually retained its hidage assessment, no doubt to facilitate the organization of bridge work, fortification, and other duties.

A more elaborate explanation of these round numbers for the *inland* assessment of the 17½ south-western hundreds of Northamptonshire is to be found in the following hypothetical reconstruction of the administrative process underlying the production of the Geld Roll. What happened, I think, was that some official at the centre, near to the king, was disappointed with the poor yield from Northamptonshire from what was possibly the very first geld levied after the Norman Conquest. Here was a shire assessed in the County Hidage at 3,200 hides, yet less than one fifth of them could be induced to pay geld. The sheriff was ordered to account for the discrepancy. At this early stage of Norman administration, he would still have been an Englishman,[2] and he prepared his report in English. He knew of two main reasons why the levy had produced less than was anticipated by the Normans from the county's nominal 3,200 hides. First, the assessment had already been reduced to 2,663 hides by the time of the Confessor—a reduction (it will be shown) which was not spread evenly over

yet the total hidage for the hundred is all accounted for in the Roll. It seems therefore that the *inland* for this hundred was given the name 'borough land'. Just as the 25-hide assessment of Northampton represents one quarter of the geld liability of the hundred of Spelhoe in which it lay, so the 50-hide assessment of Huntingdon was initially reckoned as one quarter of the geld liability of the double hundred of Hurstingstone (DB, f. 203; *VCH, Hunts.*, I, p. 338). The absence of any *inland* assessment for the remainder of Spelhoe hundred further emphasises the arbitrary nature of these figures.

[1] *VCH, Northants.*, I, p. 260.

[2] *EHD*, II, 1959, p. 430. He may have been the person called 'Northman' to whom the Confessor addressed a writ from his deathbed: see F. E. Harmer, *Anglo-Saxon Writs*, 1952, no. 94.

the shire, being confined in fact to the north-eastern hundreds. Secondly, large areas within the county had been devastated just before the Conquest.[1]

So the sheriff worked through the levies hundred by hundred. For each hundred he recorded its original assessment, and its assessment TRE. Then he listed the number of hides which had paid their geld. This, subtracted from the assessment, would give a figure for the 'waste' of each hundred; but before he could make this subtraction, the sheriff had to account for certain privileged estates which were totally exempt, and also for the baronial demesne, which was likewise exempt from the geld. For those hundreds lying in the north-eastern half of the county the precise extent of this demesne was known and recorded; very probably similar data were available for the hundreds in the remaining half, but these hundreds had not managed to secure a general reduction in their hidage assessment in the pre-Conquest period, as had the north-eastern hundreds; presumably therefore they were less easily able to pay their geld, and the sheriff agreed to some reduction in their liability, which he allowed for by inflating the total *inland* assessment up to some arbitrary round sum for each hundred.[2]

The whole record is suggestive of a retrospective piece of accounting. It was not compiled as an instrument for levying the geld; still less could it have been put together during the process of collecting the money. It is an *apologia*, a piece written after the event to explain away the small amount collected. Indeed, it would not be unreasonable to regard it as a primitive form of Inquest, although as Galbraith has pointed out[3] there is no evidence within the document that its production necessitated a full-scale *inquisitio geldi*, with commissions taking sworn evidence and producing a detailed report of the type represented by the later geld accounts of the south-western shires. The Northamptonshire Geld Roll records a less formal, single-handed investigation, by a local English official who could only have been the sheriff, or a reeve deputed by him. And this English sheriff performed his task so effectively that the Normans were convinced. Henceforth the county was to be rated at only twice the number of those hides from which the geld had been raised at this first attempt at a levy.

So ends the hypothesis; but before passing to other topics it should be mentioned that the order in which the hundreds appear in the Geld Roll merits careful study. First, the eight hundreds lying in the south-west of the county are

[1] ASC (D and E versions), *sub anno* 1065.

[2] It must be remembered also that the landowner with by far the most substantial and widespread interests in the north-eastern group of hundreds was Abbot Brand of Peterborough, who had incurred the severe displeasure of the Conqueror by his support of the aetheling Edgar (ASC, E version, *s.a.* 1066). Such a person could hardly expect from the sheriff any favour in the way of reduction of his geld assessment.

[3] Galbraith, *op. cit.*, p. 95.

Table II: The Northamptonshire Geld Roll

	Map No.	Hundred	*Number of Hides*						
			'Gewered'	'Inland'	King's land	Not paid	Waste	Accounted for	Total
8 S.W. Hundreds	I	King's Sutton	21⅔	40	10	—	28⅓	100	100
	III	Chipping Warden	17¾	40	—	—	41¼	99	100
	V	Cleyley	18	40	—	—	42	100	100
	VII	Fawsley	18½	35	5	—	41½	100	100
		(*Gravesende*)							
	II	*Eadboldestowe*	23½	45	5	—	26½	100	100
	VIII	*Egelweardesle*	16½	40	—	6½	37	100	100
	IV	Green's Norton	16	30	21	—	33	100	100
		(*Foxle*)							
	VI	Towcester	19	40	20	—	21	100	100
8 N.E. Hundreds (of Oundle)	XXIII	Huxloe	8	15	—	—	39	62	62
	XXVI	Willybrook	7	11	—	31*	13	62	62
	XXVII	Nassaburgh	50	27	—	2½	29½	109	108½
		(*Optonegrene*)†							
	XVII & XVIII	*Navereslund*†	[81½]	59	—	8	11½	—	160
	XXIV	Navisford	15	14	—	—	33	62	62
	XXV	Polebrook	10	20	—	—	32	62	62
	X	Nobottle Grove‡	44⅞	72	—	—	33⅛	150	150
	IX	Guilsborough‡	16	68	—	—	66	150	150
	XIV	Spelhoe	20½	[25] §	—	16	28½	90	90
	XXIX	W. *Hwicceslea*	10	40	—	—	30	80	80
	XXVIII	E. *Hwicceslea*	15	34	—	—	31	80	80
	XX	*Stotfalde*	9⅛	40	—	—	50⅞	100	100
	XXI	*Stoche*	17½	10½	—	—	12	40	40
	XII	Higham Ferrers‡	49½	44	—	—	56	149½‖	150
	XV	*Malesle*	12	30	8	—	30	80	80
	XXII	Corby	7½	11½	12¼¶	5	10¾	47	47
	XIX	Rothwell	10	20	—	15	[15]	45	60
	XIII	Hamfordshoe	[26]	25	—	—	39	—	90
	XVI	Orlingbury	29½	24½	—	5	21	80	80
	XI	Wymersley‡	41	60	—	—	49	150	150
		Total Hides	$630\frac{11}{12}$	960½	81¼	89	900⅚	—	2,663½

* 'Half hundred'. † Double hundred. ‡ Hundred and a half. § 'Borough land'.
‖ "And 10 hides in addition belonging to Hamfordshoe". ¶ 'Waste'.

listed. Next appear the eight hundreds lying in the extreme north-east, which formed a unit met with in earlier and later records under the name of the 'eight hundreds of Oundle'. The remaining sixteen hundreds are then listed, all jumbled up in no particular order. Clearly, these two groups of eight hundreds formed important subdivisions of the shire; they are examples of the *ferdings* so dear to Anglo-Saxon administrators. Each group had its own characteristic pattern of hidation.

The analysis of the Northants. Geld Roll on p. 20 is based on that first published by Round; some corrections have been made, using the edition of the Roll by Robertson.

THE POST-CONQUEST HIDATION OF INDIVIDUAL ESTATES

On a number of occasions, individual estates are referred to in sufficient detail in the Geld Roll for their identity to be established by cross-reference to Domesday. Comparison of the hidation in these cases provides important evidence of the way in which the post-Conquest reduction in assessment was applied to individual holdings. It must be remembered that the hidages in the Geld Roll are specifically described as being those obtaining in the time of the Confessor.

The first estates which have to be dealt with are those described in the Geld Roll as belonging to the king. When the Roll is examined carefully, it becomes apparent that in those hundreds in which the king's estates are specifically mentioned, the formulae for describing these estates fall into two distinct groups: in the first five hundreds the 'king's own farm land' appears between the *inland* and the waste; in the remaining four hundreds the king's land is said to be '*unwered*', and appears in no particular order. Moreover, all five hundreds utilizing the first formula are members of the south-western group of eight hundreds which has been referred to already. The table on p. 22 compares the hidage of the 'king's own farm land' in the Geld Roll with the total hidage of the royal estates in these eight south-western hundreds at the time of Domesday.

It will be seen that the ratio of Geld Roll hides : Domesday hides is almost exactly 5 : 2 throughout, being exactly so in the case of *Eadboldestowe*, where the estate in question is the king's manor of Whitfield. Now it will be shown that this 5 : 2 ratio represents the reduction in hidation between the dates of the Geld Roll and Domesday Book for *all* estates in the eight south-western hundreds. It follows that for this part of the county the Geld Roll includes the whole of the

Table III: The Hidage of Royal Estates

Map No.	*Hundred*	*Royal Estates in Domesday*	*Domesday Hides*	*Geld Roll Hides*	*Ratio of Geld Roll Hides : Domesday Hides*
I	King's Sutton	King's Sutton Walton Grounds (in King's Sutton) Charlton (in Newbottle)	3h $1v+\frac{1}{5}v$ $3v+\frac{1}{5}v$ *Total* $4h+\frac{2}{5}v$	10h	5:2·02
II	*Eadboldestowe*	Whitfield	2h	5h	5:2·00
III	Chipping Warden	0	0	0	0
IV	Green's Norton (*Foxle*)	Green's Norton Blakesley Adstone	$7h+1v$ (Green's Norton, Blakesley, Adstone together)	21h (IV)	
V	Cleyley	Passenham Puxley (in Passenham)	1h $\frac{1}{2}h$ *Total* $8\frac{3}{4}h$	0 (V) *Total* 21h	5:1·96
VI	Towcester	Towcester Towcester	$\frac{1}{2}h+(\frac{1}{5}\times\frac{1}{2})h$ $7\frac{1}{2}h$ *Total* $8\frac{1}{10}h$	20h	5:2·02
VII	Fawsley (*Gravesende*)	Fawsley Fawsley (King's Almsmen)	$1\frac{1}{2}h+\frac{1}{5}h$ $(\frac{4}{5}\times\frac{1}{2})h$ *Total* $2\frac{1}{10}h$	5h	5:2·10
VIII	*Egelweardesle*	0	0	0	0

royal estates within each hundred in its description of 'the king's own farm land'.

Turning to the rest of the county, in the few cases where there are specific references within the roll to estates held by the king and 'the lady' his wife, these cannot be identified with sufficient certainty for useful comparison in the cases of *Malesle*, Corby, Rothwell, and *Navereslund* hundreds; but the statement in the Geld Roll that the king held half the hundred of Willybrook, amounting to 31 hides, is borne out by the Domesday hidation of the king's estates in that hundred, which amounts to the unusually high figure of 16h + 2½v. Together with the 3-hide estate held by Eustace the sheriff, which was possibly once a royal estate, this gives a total of 19h + 2½v, almost precisely half the Domesday total of 39h for the hundred.[1]

It will be shown later that at the time of Domesday, the demesne of the king's estates throughout the county was not only exempt from the geld: usually it was not even hidated. The Geld Roll reveals that in the case of the eight south-western hundreds, the parts of the royal estates which were not held in demesne—the *warland*, or land farmed by the estate villeins for themselves—were hidated, but exempt from the geld. For the remainder of the county this was not generally the case, although there were a few exceptions; apart from these, one assumes that the non-demesne portions of the royal estates paid geld in the same fashion as the rest of the estates in each hundred.

There are a few references in the roll to estates held by persons other than the king, but which were nevertheless specially privileged by being wholly exempt from the geld. In the hundred of *Egelweardesle* an estate of 6½h at Norton, then tenanted by Osmund, the king's secretary, falls within this category. This must surely be the estate at Norton held of the king by the Count of Meulan at the time of Domesday, when it was assessed at 2½h plus ($\frac{1}{5} \times \frac{1}{2}$)h (i.e. exactly $\frac{2}{5}$ of 6½h); formerly, says Domesday, it was held by *Agemund* freely. It may be that DB *Agemund* is a mistake for Osmund here.

William Engaine was the king's huntsman, which was no doubt the reason

[1] It will be seen that I do not follow R. S. Hoyt in his elaborate comparison of the hidation of the royal estates in DB and the Northants. Geld Roll (*The Royal Demesne in English Constitutional History: 1066–1272*, pp. 59–63). Hoyt's analysis rests upon two general assumptions, the first unproven and the second untenable: (a) that "the *caput* of a scattered estate paid the geld assessed upon its members in several hundreds" (*ibid.*, p. 41, n. 80); and (b) that for any Northants. DB holding, subtraction of the figure given for the number of *ploughs* on the demesne, from the figure given for the number of plough teams for which there is land (the *ploughlands*), gives the number of 'Domesday non-demesne ploughlands', or the 'warland' to use Hoyt's terminology (*ibid.*, p. 44). The Geld Roll does not easily lend itself to an interpretation which supports Hoyt's first assumption; as for the second, Round showed long ago that the number of *ploughs* on either the demesne or the villein's holdings has nothing to do with the number of *ploughlands* recorded for each estate in the Northamptonshire section of Domesday; this latter figure is clearly a unit of assessment, whereas the former actually records the number of ploughs in use on each estate. Hoyt's table is therefore unsound, and *ipso facto* any conclusion he draws from it.

why his estates, together with those of his brother Richard, were exempt from the geld in the year recorded by the Northamptonshire Geld Roll.[1] Here again, it is instructive to compare the Geld Roll and Domesday hidation of the estates concerned:

Table IV: Hidage of the Engaine Fief

Tenant	*Hundred*	*Estate*	*Geld Roll hidage*	*Domesday hidage*
Richard Engaine	Spelhoe	Abington	10h	4h
William Engaine*	Spelhoe	Moulton	6h	2h+1½v
William Engaine	Orlingbury	Pytchley	5h	2h
Richard Engaine	Nassaburgh	Stibbington	2½h	2h

* As sub-tenant of Robert de Buci.

In the first three cases, in the hundreds of Spelhoe and Orlingbury, the reduction in hidage conforms with the ratio 5:2. For the estate lying in Nassaburgh hundred, however, the ratio is 2½:2, or 5:4. The significance of this will appear later.

THE HIDE AND THE PLOUGHLAND[2]

The most interesting feature of the county's hidation is undoubtedly the relationship recorded in Domesday between the hidage of each individual

[1] Round, *Feudal England*, pp. 154–6.

[2] The term 'ploughland' is adopted here in preference to 'teamland', which is used by J. S. Moore in his recent discussion of this topic ('The Domesday Teamland: a Reconsideration', in *Transactions of the Royal Historical Society*, 5th series, XIV, 1964, pp. 109–30). Mr Moore concluded that "the teamlands . . . normally measure land actually occupied and cultivated in 1086", but the detailed statistics for the Northamptonshire hundreds which appear as an Appendix to the present paper demonstrate that this claim cannot possibly hold good for the whole of Northamptonshire, for the hide: ploughland ratios are too artificial, those of Wymersley hundred being particularly notable in this respect. Similarly artificial figures for Domesday ploughlands occur very frequently throughout the Northern Danelaw, and also in Bedfordshire; in Huntingdonshire and Cambridgeshire, however, and in many southern and western shires, such artificiality is not so easily demonstrable. One is forced to agree with Professor Darby's conclusion (*Domesday Geography of Eastern England*, 1954, p. 42) that the Domesday jurors' concept of the ploughland varied from place to place. Whether or not the Domesday ploughlands represent 'agricultural reality' in the rest of England, it is my conviction that in the Danelaw they are more closely related to an assessment for tribute (and probably for other obligations such as bridge and fortress work) imposed by each earl on the territory allotted to members of his *here*, soon after the Danish settlement of 877. The Domesday carucates represent the assessment operative at the time of the Survey; where the carucate figures differ from the ploughland figures, this is due to a reduction in assessment in the interim period. This is too large a topic for all its implications to be worked out in the present paper.

estate and the number of ploughs for which that estate is said to have sufficient land. In the Northants. section of Domesday, these 'ploughlands' have little or nothing to do with the actual number of ploughs employed on each estate; they are obviously artificial units of assessment, and the question we have to ask ourselves is this: do the Domesday ploughlands of south Northamptonshire, as J. H. Round asserted, represent an early stage in the hidation of the shire?[1]

This brings us face to face with the problem of the reduction of hidage assessment in Northamptonshire. The assessment recorded in the County Hidage is 3,200 hides, made up as the Geld Roll demonstrates of three 'double' hundreds (each of 200 hides), four 'hundreds and a half' (each of 150 hides), and 20 ordinary hundreds of 100 hides. But the Geld Roll also supplies the figure of 2,663½ for the total hidage of the shire at the time of the Norman Conquest; and the total hidage recorded in Domesday, some twenty years later, is only 1,244.

Against this we must set the total number of ploughlands recorded in Domesday for the county, which amounts to 2,728⅜, giving an average of 85¼ ploughlands per hundred. More precise analysis shows that for the eight south-western hundreds there are recorded 754¼ ploughlands, or an average of 94¼ per hundred, while for the 24 hundreds remaining there are only 1,974¼ ploughlands, or an average of 82¼ per hundred.

It is necessary to investigate this topic still further, helped by statistics of the Domesday hidage and ploughland assessments of the shire, hundred by hundred, recorded *in extenso* in the Appendix to this paper. We may commence our summary of the situation so revealed with a general statement that whereas the 14½ hundreds in the south-western end of the county all show a fixed relationship between the hidage and ploughland assessments of their constituent estates, no such relationship is discernible in the 17½ hundreds forming the north-eastern portion of Northamptonshire.

Moreover, the hundreds of the first half may be further subdivided into the group of eight in the extreme south-west, already referred to above, in which the hide: ploughland ratio is 2:5, and a group of six and a half hundreds surrounding the town of Northampton, in which (with one exception) the ratio 1h:2p obtains. These groups will now be taken in turn for further discussion.

Group A (1): The Eight Hundreds in the Extreme South-West

These are numbered I–VIII on the accompanying map, and perusal of the assessments shows a very characteristic pattern for six of these hundreds; the ratio here is 2h: 5p, and the 4-hide unit is prevalent. Where vills are divided between two or more owners, the hidage is given usually in fractions of one-fifth.

[1] *EHR*, xv, 1900, p. 83.

Two hundreds within the group, namely IV Green's Norton (*Foxle*) and V Cleyley, are anomalous in that although each is assessed in 4-hide units, with fractions of $\frac{1}{5}$ hide in the case of divided vills, they do not individually show the same 2h: 5p ratio as do other members of the group. However, when the assessments for these two hundreds are added together, the resultant total approaches the 2h: 5p ratio, as will be seen in the table below:

IV Green's Norton (*Foxle*)	33h	66p
V Cleyley	41h+1a	129½p
totals	74h+1a	195½p
ratio	2h: 5·37p	

One can only assume that the hidage assessment was imposed on these two hundreds jointly.

This 2h: 5p relationship was first discovered by J. H. Round, but he was unable to delimit the area for which it holds good. There seems no alternative to Round's hypothesis concerning these assessments; for those Northamptonshire hundreds lying wholly or partly to the south-west of Watling Street, evidently the ploughland figure of each individual estate represents its hidation at the time of Edward the Elder, if not before. Why then should the Domesday jurors still remember these assessments, and why should the Domesday commissioners seek out and record this information? The answer, I submit, is that the post-Conquest reduction in Northamptonshire's hidation was essentially one of geld liability only; the other obligations of bridge and fortress work remained unabated, and the 'ploughland' figures were required to preserve the estate assessments for these duties. For each assessment unit, so many feet of wall in the nearest *burh* must be maintained, and so many feet of the county's bridges and causeways must be repaired. Originally the assessment covered also service in the *fyrd*, but the whole structure of army service was changed radically soon after the Conquest, as a result of which the late Anglo-Saxon assessment units throughout the country were relieved of their liability for this particular burden.

Group A (2): The Six and a half Hundreds surrounding Northampton

With one exception these all show the ratio 1h: 2p. They can be subdivided as follows:

1. Hundreds in which the assessments are in 4-hide units: Guilsborough and Nobottle Grove (each 1½ hundreds), Hamfordshoe and Spelhoe (map nos. IX, X, XIII, and XIV).

2. Hundred in which the assessments are in $3\frac{1}{2}$-hide units: Wymersley ($1\frac{1}{2}$ hundreds).[1] This exceptional hundred has a very strong $3\frac{1}{2}$h:9p ratio (map no. XI).

The significance of these ratios will be discussed later.

Group B: The Seventeen and a half North-Eastern Hundreds of Northamptonshire

In none of these hundreds can there be demonstrated a simple relationship between the Domesday hidation and the ploughland assessments. A subdivision is possible, however, on a hidage basis:

1. Hundreds with 5- and 10-hide units: North and South *Navereslund*, Polebrook, Navisford, and Corby (map nos. XVII, XVIII, XXV, XXIV, and XXII).
2. Hundreds with 3-hide units: Willybrook, Nassaburgh, Higham Ferrers, and Huxloe (map nos. XXVI, XXVII, XII, and XXIII).
3. Hundreds with $4\frac{3}{4}$-hide units: *Malesle* and Orlingbury (map nos. XV and XVI).[2]
4. Hundreds in which the hidage assessments are strongly fractionated in thirds: *Stotfalde*, *Stoche*, and Rothwell. Of these, *Stoche* has a regular pattern of 4-hide units, but the adjacent hundreds of Rothwell and *Stotfalde* do not appear to have their constituent estates arranged in any regular hidage pattern (map nos. XX, XXI, and XIX).
5. Hundreds in which the hidage assessments have no discernible characteristic features: the two hundreds of *Hwicceslea* (map nos. XXVIII and XXIX).

J. H. Round, who first established that a duodecimal system underlies the geld assessment of the carucated shires, was also the first to suggest that the ploughlands in north-east Northamptonshire follow a similar duodecimal pattern, i.e. the individual assessments are usually divisible by 3 or 4.[3] This is particularly well marked in the hundreds of Nassaburgh, Willybrook, Polebrook, Huxloe, and Corby, but to some extent it is characteristic of all the hundreds in Group B.

The assessments for East and West *Hwicceslea* (which later formed part of Rutland) are duodecimal like the rest in the group (as suggested by Sir Frank Stenton),[4] but it seems to me that the vills can be grouped topographically in a more satisfactory manner by supposing that they were assessed also in multiples of seven. It was not until I had arranged the vills of these two hundreds in

[1] First detected by F. Baring, using the hidation of the Northants. Survey: *EHR*, XVII, pp. 81–2; he did not, however, discover the assessment unit of nine ploughlands for this hundred, here described for the first time.

[2] First detected by Baring, *ibid.*, p. 82.

[3] *VCH, Northants.*, I, p. 266.

[4] *VCH, Rutland*, I, p. 126.

this fashion, that I found on examination of the DB assessments for the remaining portion of Rutland that the ploughlands of Alstoe Wapentake are grouped in two 'hundreds' of 42 units each, and that the king's three demesne manors in Martinsley Wapentake were assessed together at 14 ploughlands. It has already been postulated that East and West *Hwicceslea* were originally part of a territory dependent on the Danish borough of Stamford. It may now be suggested that Alstoe and Martinsley Wapentakes were also once part of this territory (for they had the same carucation pattern) and that when the county of Rutland was formed after Domesday, the Normans were in fact reconstituting part of a Danish unit of local administration.

THE PLOUGHLANDS: A NEW HYPOTHESIS

We are now in a position to suggest an answer to the question posed earlier on. The pattern of Domesday ploughland assessment is decimal for the hundreds forming Group A (1), and duodecimal for those of Group B. The pattern in Group A (2) was also initially decimal, but at some stage most of the 10p units secured a reduction to 8p (or to 9p in the case of Wymersley). Round's hypothesis, that the ploughland assessments represent an early stage in the (post-Danish) hidation of the shire, applies therefore only to the south-western half of the county; for the other half, with its duodecimal pattern, we must postulate that the ploughland figures represent the Danish carucation. For all except the ancient royal estates (which are dealt with separately below), these Domesday ploughland assessments record the liability of the estate for bridge and fortress work; the geld liability is recorded by the hidage allocated to each estate.

THE PLOUGHLAND ASSESSMENT OF CROWN HOLDINGS

Another important factor which has to be taken into account when considering Round's hypothesis is the high assessment given for the ploughlands of the king's royal estates. For the total of all types of estates in the county, the ratio of hides to ploughlands at the time of Domesday is 1,244:2,728$\frac{3}{8}$, or 1h: 2·19p. For the royal estates alone, however, the ratio is 1h: 2·73p. In other words, there were 25 per cent more ploughlands per hide on the king's estates than on those of the county taken as a whole. The more ancient the royal holding, the greater the disparity. Consider the figures for the following royal estates:

Tixover	2h 8p	Duddington	1h 8p	Kingsthorpe	$4\frac{3}{4}$h 20p
Towcester	$7\frac{1}{2}$h 22p	Rothwell	$8\frac{3}{4}$h 40p	Nassington	6h 16p
Gretton	$3\frac{3}{4}$h 14p	Brixworth	$9\frac{1}{2}$h 35p	Kings Cliff	$1\frac{1}{2}$h + $\frac{1}{2}$v 14p
Corby	$1\frac{1}{2}$h 9p	Faxton	2h 12p	Passenham	1h 12p

Of these, Towcester and Passenham were royal *burhs* in the time of Edward the Elder. Corby and Rothwell gave their names to their respective hundreds, and so (on one occasion in DB) did Gretton; and Dr Cam has shown that this fashion of naming a hundred after a royal vill was in vogue in the tenth century. Brixworth has a notable early church, and could well have been a royal vill from the time of its re-conquest by Edward the Elder. We have here, it seems, something we possess for no other county: an easy way of distinguishing in Domesday between ancient Crown holdings of the early tenth century, and those acquired by the king at some time nearer to the Norman Conquest, e.g. by forfeiture. These later acquisitions, whose hide:ploughland ratios are indistinguishable from those of non-royal estates in the same hundreds, were often made appurtenant to the ancient Crown estates, as the following examples taken from Domesday will show:

*Table V: Crown Holdings at Domesday**

Ancient estates			*Attached estates*		
Upton	2h	10p	Harleston	$\frac{1}{2}$h	2p
Corby	$1\frac{1}{2}$h	9p	Stoke Albany	1h	2p
Passenham	1h	12p	Puxley	$\frac{1}{2}$h	1p
Kingsthorpe	$4\frac{3}{4}$h	20p	Moulton Weston	$1\frac{5}{8}$h 1h	5p
Rothwell	$8\frac{3}{4}$h	40p	Loddington, Clendon, Draughton, Arthingworth, Desborough, Kelmarsh, Oxendon, Clipston, Cransley, Broughton	10h	19p

* In this table, the estates in the right-hand column were attached at the time of Domesday to the corresponding estates of the left-hand column.

Why should there be this great disparity between the hidage and the ploughland figures for the ancient royal estates? One explanation might be that they received 'beneficial hidation', i.e. a privileged reduction in assessment. But this reduction was not, it seems, applied to the whole of each estate. Careful examination of the assessments leads me to the opinion that whereas the ploughland figures for the royal estates represent both the demesne (or *inland*) and the villein holdings (or *warland*) of the estate, the hidage figures apply only to the *warland*; i.e. the Crown *inland* was not hidated in Northamptonshire at the time of Domesday, and indeed it was probably not hidated at the time of the imposition of the post-Danish hidage assessment. This offers what seems to me to be the only satisfactory explanation of the position in those hundreds (*Eadboldestowe*, Towcester, and Nobottle Grove) where all but the ancient Crown holdings show a fixed relationship between hides and ploughlands.

This theory concerning the hidation of the Crown *inland* receives powerful support when one examines the descriptions of those estates in the Northamptonshire Domesday in which the word *inland* is mentioned specifically. Only three estates fall within this category; all were Crown holdings in the south-western half of the county and they appear as consecutive entries, the relevant portions of which may be summarized as follows:[1]

> Whitfield in *Eadboldestowe* hundred: "there are 2 hides, and *inland* for 2 ploughs, and for the men land for 5 ploughs."
> Fawsley in *Gravesende* hundred: "there are 1½ hides and the fifth part of a hide. There is *inland* for 4 ploughs; there are 2 ploughs [there]. And 6 bordars with [land for] 4 ploughs [are] on the other land outside the demesne, and 6 villeins and a reeve have 4 ploughs [there]."
> Hardingstone in Wymersley hundred: "there are 5 hides, besides the *inland* [where there] is land for 4 ploughs. There are 2 ploughs [on the *inland*] and 4 villeins and 10 bordars have 4 ploughs [on the other land]."

The Domesday passages are made difficult because the clerk left out whole words which were not necessary at the time, for no doubt the meaning was clear enough to his contemporaries. They are supplied—conjecturally, one must admit—in square brackets in the version of the entries given above.

This habit of assessing the *inland* in ploughlands, and the remainder of the estate in hides, is met with elsewhere in Domesday descriptions of estates, both within and outside the Danelaw, in which the *inland* is exempt from the geld.[2] The classic example is to be found in the Huntingdonshire section of the survey, where there is a general statement that "in Hurstingstone hundred, demesne

[1] DB, f. 219 b; *VCH, Northants*, I, p. 305.

[2] The best factual summary of the position known to me appears in R. Weldon Finn's *An Introduction to Domesday Book*, 1963, pp. 258–61.

ploughlands are quit from the King's geld."[1] One finds the following typical entries relating to Ramsey Abbey estates in this hundred:[2]

"In Stukeley the abbey had 7 hides assessed to the geld. There is land for 11 ploughs. Apart from these hides, the abbey has land for 2 ploughs in demesne."

"In Abbots Ripton the abbey had 10 hides assessed to the geld. There is land for 16 ploughs, and there is land for 2 ploughs in demesne, apart from the aforesaid hides."

"In Wistow the abbey had 9 hides assessed to the geld. There is land for 16 ploughs, and the abbey has land for 3 ploughs in demesne, apart from the aforesaid hides."

The same distinction is to be found in the Burton Abbey surveys of the early twelfth century, for which the following entries may be quoted as typical examples:[3]

"In Burton there is *inland* for 2 ploughs. There are 2 ploughs with 16 oxen... The land of the men is assessed at 1½ hides."

"In Branston there is half a hide of *inland* which can be ploughed by 3 ploughs. Now there are 2, with 16 oxen... The land of the men is assessed at 1½ hides."

"In Stretton there is as much *inland* as can be served by 3 ploughs. Now there are 2, with 16 oxen... The land of the men is assessed to the geld at 1½ hides."

It will be noted that only in one case is the *inland* hidated; the usual way of assessing it is in ploughlands.

It is apparent, therefore, that part of the explanation of the relatively high ploughland assessments (or, more precisely, accepting Round's hypothesis, the relatively low hidage assessments) of the ancient Crown estates in Northamptonshire at the time of Domesday could be that at some time during the century and a half before the Norman Conquest, the Crown *inland* in Northamptonshire lost its original hidation. This state of affairs could only have arisen following the long-continued exemption of the *inland* from the geld and other obligations. Once the Crown *inland* became exempt from these duties, there was no point in remembering its hidage; a more useful (though still nominal) assessment was the number of ploughs which it could maintain. The marked difference between Domesday hide: ploughland ratios for the earliest Crown holdings and those of the estates acquired by the Crown at a period much nearer to the Conquest, gives good ground for assuming that the Crown demesne in Northamptonshire secured its exemption from the geld and other duties at the time of, or not long after, the second hidation of the county, i.e. some time in the second quarter of the tenth century.

[1] DB, f. 203; *VCH, Hunts.*, I, p. 338. [2] DB, f. 204; *VCH, Hunts.*, I, pp. 342–3. [3] *EHD*, II, pp. 821–2.

The general correspondence between the hidation figures of the County Hidage and those of Domesday prevents us from assuming that this process necessarily occurred at so early a date on the royal estates in other counties. But the evidence relating to Ramsey and Burton which has been presented above, together with the well-known writ of Edward the Confessor to Bury St Edmunds,[1] suggests that the exemption of *inland* from the geld and other duties was extended to the estates of some monasteries in the late Anglo-Saxon period, and that by the time of the Norman Conquest the precedent was sufficiently well established in these cases for the *inland* to have lost its original hidation. After the Conquest the privilege was applied more generally, so that the demesnes of baronial estates everywhere became exempt from the geld, although their hidage assessments were retained, probably to facilitate the organization of work on bridges and fortifications.

Returning to the matter of the royal *inland* of Northamptonshire, it must be stressed that its relief from geld liabilities offers only a partial explanation of the high Domesday ploughland assessments of the ancient Crown estates within the shire. It cannot possibly account for the whole of the disparity between the hidage and the ploughland figures of these estates; nor may one assume that the remaining part of this disparity arose from some later and more general beneficial hidation of Northamptonshire Crown lands, for the pattern of hidation and ploughland assessments of the individual hundreds cannot be manipulated to fit such a theory. After much contemplation of this thorny problem I have arrived at the hypothesis that the Domesday ploughland figures for the ancient royal estates of Northamptonshire represent in fact their initial, pre-Danish hidation, and that this early assessment was preserved by Edward the Elder solely as an index of the special liabilities of these estates for their share of the royal food farm; alongside this primitive figure he allocated a new hidage assessment to cover geld and (possibly) other public liabilities.

THE PRE-CONQUEST HIDATION OF INDIVIDUAL ESTATES

In the table on page 33 I have listed all known charter and narrative references to the pre-Conquest hidation of estates in Northamptonshire, and compared them with the hidation given in Domesday. Only in a very few cases, however, is it safe to assume that the estates have the same bounds at the two different periods. Most unfortunately, the county is very poorly endowed with pre-Conquest charters.

[1] F. Harmer, *Anglo-Saxon Writs*, 1952, p. 139.

Table VI: Pre-Conquest Hidation of Estates

Hundred Map No.	*Hundred*	*Source**	*Estate*	*Date*	*Charter hidage*	*DB hidage*	*Remarks*
VII	Fawsley (*Gravesende*)	*CS* 986	Stowe	956	5h	4h	bounds
VIII	*Egelweardesle*	*CS* 792	Badby	944	30h	12h	bounds; original charter
		CS 978	Braunston	956	8h	$3\frac{3}{4}$h	bounds; original charter
		K 736	Newnham	1021–3	5h	—	bounds
XI	Wymersley	*Chron. Rams.* p. 117	Denton	991	1h	3h (with Whiston)	part only
XII	Higham Ferrers	*CS* 1297	Irchester	963–73	2h	$2h + 3\frac{1}{2}h$	two DB estates
XVIII	N. *Navereslund*	*CS* 943	Kettering	956	10h	10h	bounds
		CS 815	Warkton	946	10h	4h	same estate?
XXII	Corby	*Chron. Rams.* pp. 74–5	Boughton House in Weekley	975–9	1h	$\frac{1}{2}h + 1h$	two DB estates
		Chron. Rams. pp. 76–8	Oakley	*c.* 987	8h	$1\frac{1}{2}h + \frac{1}{2}v$	
		Chron. Rams. pp. 76–8	Weekley	*c.* 987	10h	5h	
XXIII	Huxloe	*Chron. Rams.* pp. 76–8	Barnwell	*c.* 987	18h	$6h + 6\frac{1}{4}h$	two DB estates
		K 1308	Twywell	1013	$3\frac{1}{2}$h	$3h - 1\frac{1}{2}v$	bounds
XXIV	Navisford	*CS* 1297	Titchmarsh	*c.* 973	$1\frac{1}{2}h + \frac{1}{2}h + 1h$	3h + 1v(?)	
XXV	Polebrook	R XL	Ashton	*c.* 984	1h	$4\frac{1}{2}$h	part only?
XXVI	Willybrook	R XL	Lutton	*c.* 984	$1\frac{1}{2}$h	$2\frac{1}{2}$h	part only?
		R XL	Warmington	*c.* 984	1h	1h	same estate?
XXVII	Nassaburgh (*Optonegrene*)	*CS* 871	Ailsworth	948	3h	3h + 6h	bounds; two DB estates
		R XL	Thorpe	*c.* 984	3h	2h	part only?
		R XL	Wittering	*c.* 984	1h — 1 oxgang	9h	part only?

Clearly, useful comparison can be made only when the pre-Conquest source is a charter of established authenticity, in which the bounds are given, and when it can be proved that the bounds of the estate did not change between the date of the charter and the time of Domesday. In practice this means that the charter bounds must be traceable on estate maps or ordnance maps, and shown to be identical with later parish bounds. The number of cases in the above list which meet these criteria is small indeed. The only examples worthy of discussion are those of Stowe, Badby, Braunston, Ailsworth, Kettering, and Twywell.

In the case of Kettering we have a twelfth-century copy of what purports to be a charter of A.D. 956. Its formulae and witness list stand up to all the conventional tests of authenticity. The bounds are identical with those of the later parish,[1] and the holding is assessed at 10 hides both in the charter and in the Domesday Survey. But we know that between these two dates, the hidage of the hundred of North *Navereslund* in which Kettering lay had been reduced from 80 hides to 36¼ hides. It seems unlikely that Kettering could have retained its original hidage throughout this period. One might suggest that the copyist, while transcribing the original charter into his cartulary, found within the charter a hidage assessment for Kettering grossly in excess of the Domesday assessment for the estate, and in his transcript silently reduced the charter assessment to the Domesday figure. The hypothesis gains strength when one recalls that the Domesday assessment for Kettering was the same at the time of the Northants. Survey, some fifty years later, and therefore at the time the clerk was entering the charter in his cartulary. A similar course of events could have occurred in the case of the Ailsworth charter,[2] which appears in the same cartulary.

For Twywell, the reduction in hidage between the time of the charter (1013) and Domesday is exactly 25 per cent.[3] The general reduction for the hundred within which it lay is in the order of 50 per cent between the time of the Confessor and Domesday. For Stowe, the reduction between 956 and 1086 is 20 per cent, against 60 per cent for its parent hundred in the same period.[4] In neither case are the charters concerned originals, and the possibility cannot be overlooked that the hidage figures in the surviving versions have been tampered with. But it would be wrong to pass on without the admission that the evidence they appear to offer runs counter to the main argument here presented—a situation which is very disturbing. It is to be hoped that further analysis will one day clear up this discrepancy.

When we come to the surviving original Anglo-Saxon charters of Northamptonshire, however, the evidence is firm and convincing. The charter for

[1] *P.N, Northants.*, p. 184, n. 1. [2] *Ibid.*, p. 228, n. 1. [3] *Ibid.*, p. 188, n. 1. [4] *Ibid.*, p. 30, n. 1.

Braunston is dated 956; the bounds have been worked out in detail, and can be shown to be substantially the same as those of the modern parish.[1] The hidage given in the charter is 8, while the figure in Domesday for the same estate is 3¾, a reduction of 53 per cent. Braunston lay within the hundred of *Egelweardesle*, which secured as a whole a reduction in hidation of 60 per cent over the same period.

For Badby the reduction can be shown to be exactly what one would expect theoretically, but the estate conveyed in the charter of 944 was a large one embracing four later parishes, and therefore an elaborate analysis is required to explain its hidage reduction.

THE BADBY CHARTER

CS 792 is an original charter, dated 944, conveying 30 hides at Badby, Dodford, and Everdon. The bounds are worked out in *The Place-Names of Northamptonshire*, p. 10, n. 1 (probably by F. M. Stenton), where it is shown conclusively that the estate conveyed comprised the territory within the outer limits of the four modern parishes of Badby, Newnham, Dodford, and Everdon. Newnham is not mentioned by name in this charter, but it occurs as a 5-hide estate in a charter of 1021–3 (K 736), of which the original is not preserved; the bounds are coterminous with those of the modern parish of Newnham.[2] K 1356 is a perambulation of the outer limits of Badby, Newnham, and Dodford, but omitting Everdon; the hidage is not given, and the date probably lies somewhere between those of *CS* 792 and K 736. K 1316 is a late forgery modelled on K 736, purporting to be dated 1020–3, and to convey four hides at Badby.[3] It is noteworthy that the hidage there given is the same as the Domesday hidage of Badby.

In attempting to compare the hidage of the 944 charter with that given for its constituent estates at the time of Domesday, one immediately encounters the difficulty that Newnham is not mentioned by that name, either in Domesday or in the Northamptonshire Survey. Badby and Dodford appear under *Egelweardesle* hundred, and Everdon appears under Fawsley (*Gravesende*) hundred. The rest of the Domesday estates in these two hundreds can all be accounted for on a modern map, with the exception of *Chelverdescote* in Fawsley, a lost Domesday estate which could not be located by J. H. Round, although he did suggest that from its position in the Northants. Survey, it lay somewhere near

[1] *Ibid.*, pp. 14–15, n. 1. [2] *Ibid.*, p. 26, n. 1.

[3] *Encomium Emmae Reginae*, ed. A. Campbell, Royal Historical Society, Camden 3rd Series, LXXII, 1949, p. 60.

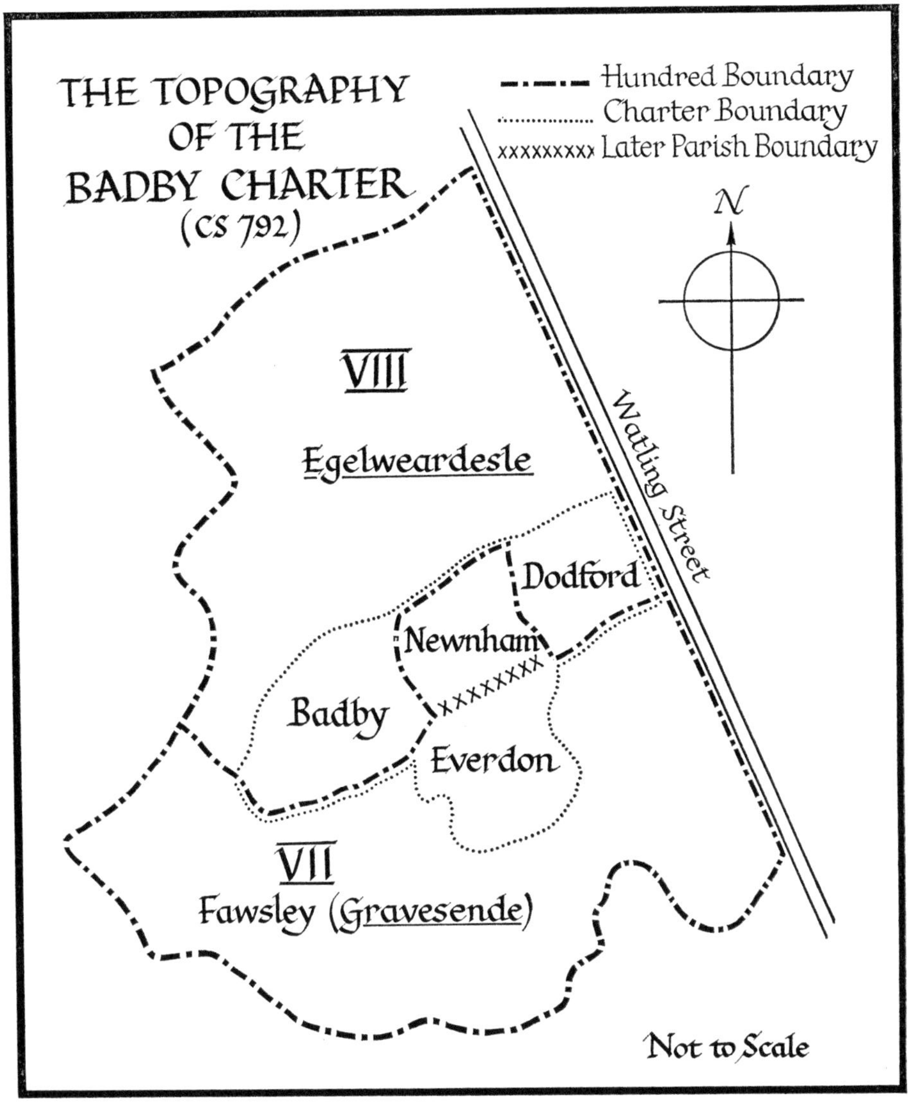
THE TOPOGRAPHY
OF THE
BADBY CHARTER
(CS 792)
Hundred Boundary
Charter Boundary
Later Parish Boundary
N
Watling Street
VIII
Egelweardesle
Dodford
Newnham
Badby
Everdon
VII
Fawsley (Gravesende)
Not to Scale

Everdon.[1] There can be little doubt that *Chelverdescote* is in fact an alternative name for Newnham, which must therefore have been in Fawsley hundred at the time of Domesday, although later it was included in the hundred of *Egelweardesle*.

We are now in a position to reconstruct the Domesday account of the estates conveyed in the Badby Charter, as follows:

Fawsley (*Gravesende*) Hundred	Count of Mortain	*Chelverdescote* (Newnham)					4h			10p	
	Bishop of Bayeux	Everdon		½h					1p		
	Count of Mortain	Snorscombe in Everdon	1½v	½h	1h	4h	12h	1p	10p	30p	
	Count of Mortain	Snorscombe in Everdon	½v						1p		
Egelweardesle Hundred	Count of Mortain	Dodford			3h				7p		
	Crowland	Badby					4h			10p	

We have therefore a total Domesday hidage of 12, with land for 30 ploughs, and it will be noted that the 4h:10p ratio is maintained for the combined estates of Everdon and Dodford, although the individual holdings vary somewhat in detail. Furthermore, the ploughlands equal the hidage of 944, but Newnham had suffered a 50 per cent reduction of hidage between that date and 1021–3. Since the Geld Roll specifically states that the hundreds of *Egelweardesle* and Fawsley (*Gravesende*) were still rated at 100 hides each TRE, this reduction in Newnham's hidage must have been the result of some internal re-allocation of hidage among the constituent estates of the Badby Charter.

HIDATION AT DIFFERENT PERIODS

We are approaching the point at which a general reconstruction of the county's hidage assessments during the century and a half preceding Domesday Book can be attempted. One further table should be studied at this juncture, in which the Geld Roll assessments for each hundred may be compared with the hundredal ploughland and hidage assessments reconstructed from Domesday. It will be seen that whereas in the time of the Confessor the hidage assigned to each hundred (according to the Northants. Geld Roll) showed a marked regional variation, by the time of Domesday this had been ironed out

[1] *VCH, Northants.*, I, p. 322, n. I.

Table VII: Hidation at Different Periods

Map No.	*Hundred*	*Hidage: Basic Hundredal Assessment*	*Hidage TRE: Geld Roll Assessment*	*Domesday Ploughlands*	*Domesday Hides*	*Northants. Survey Hides*
I	King's Sutton	100	100	$95\frac{1}{4}$	39+9a	$41\frac{7}{10}$
II	*Eadboldestowe*	100	100	$99\frac{1}{2}$	39+80a	$38\frac{3}{10}$
III	Chipping Warden	100	100	$92\frac{1}{2}$	39+90a	41
IV	Green's Norton (*Foxle*)	100	100	66	33	$40\frac{1}{2}$
V	Cleley	100	100	$129\frac{1}{2}$	41+1a	36
VI	Towcester	100	100	$94\frac{1}{2}$	38+84a	40
VII	Fawsley (*Gravesende*)	100	100	87	[35+15a]	$40\frac{7}{10}$
VIII	*Egelweardesle*	100	100	90	37+60a	$39\frac{5}{20}$
IX	Guilsborough	150	150	111	54+50a	$61\frac{7}{8}$
X	Nobottle Grove	150	150	$137\frac{3}{4}$	57+50a	$62\frac{3}{20}$
XI	Wymersley	150	150	$139\frac{1}{2}$	64+105a	$61\frac{5}{8}$
XII	Higham Ferrers	150	150	$94\frac{1}{2}$	64+45a	$60\frac{33}{40}$
XIII	Hamfordshoe	100	90	$78\frac{1}{8}$	36+45a	$36\frac{4}{10}$
XIV	Spelhoe	100	90	$106\frac{1}{2}$	47+45a	$35\frac{4}{10}$
XV	*Malesle*	100	80	83	32+105a	$40\frac{1}{2}$
XVI	Orlingbury	100	80	67	38+30a	$28\frac{7}{8}$
XVII	S. *Navereslund*	100 }	160	$67\frac{1}{2}$ } $138\frac{1}{2}$	36+90a } 73	$40\frac{17}{20}$
XVIII	N. *Navereslund*	100 }		71 }	36+30a }	$44\frac{7}{8}$
XIX	Rothwell	100	60	$98\frac{1}{2}$	37+80a	$40\frac{1}{16}$
XX	*Stotfalde*	100	100	$66\frac{1}{4}$	34+40a	39
XXI	*Stoche*	100	40	$80\frac{1}{2}$	39+83a	$41\frac{1}{6}$
XXII	Corby	100	47	118	40+15a	$38\frac{3}{8}$
XXIII	Huxloe	100	62	73	40	$38\frac{1}{2}$
XXIV	Navisford	100	62	72	42+85a	$35\frac{17}{24}$
XXV	Polebrook	100	62	$68\frac{1}{2}$	40+60a	$30\frac{19}{24}$
XXVI	Willybrook	100	62	114	39	$43\frac{5}{8}$
XXVII	Nassaburgh (*Optonegrene*)	200	$108\frac{1}{2}$	149	81+30a	$79\frac{3}{4}$
XXVIII	E. *Hwicceslea*	100	80	91	43 }	80*
XXIX	W. *Hwicceslea*	100	80	$87\frac{1}{2}$	33 }	
	Totals for Northamptonshire	3,200	$2{,}663\frac{1}{2}$	2,728[illegible]	1,244+7a	1,260†

* From the 1131 Pipe Roll.

† Compare Round, in *EHR*, xv, 1900, p. 83: "The pipe roll of 1130 implies an aggregate hidage of $1{,}192\frac{3}{4}$."

completely, and the hundreds were assessed with remarkable consistency at around 40 hides. Where this figure is departed from to any appreciable extent, there is good reason to suspect alterations in the hundredal boundaries—e.g. between Green's Norton and Cleyley, and between Hamfordshoe, Spelhoe, and *Malesle*. That these supposed alterations were only temporary[1] is shown by the figures for these hundreds obtained from the Northants. Survey.

THE CHANGING PATTERN OF HIDATION

An attempt will now be made to draw together all the material and conclusions presented above, and to summarize the way in which the county's hidage assessment was modified between the times of Edward the Elder and William the Conqueror. The case is presented dogmatically to save space, but it must be remembered that what follows is only a hypothesis, based though it is on a very detailed analysis of the evidence.

The second hidation of Northamptonshire was imposed by Edward the Elder or (less probably) by his son Athelstan, some time between 917 and 937.[2] The county assessment of 3,200 hides was distributed between 20 hundreds of 100 hides, four 'hundreds and a half' of 150 hides, and three double hundreds of 200 hides; of these double hundreds, two were divided into east and west (*Hwicceslea*) or north and south (*Navereslund*) portions, each of 100 hides. Moreover the shire contained within itself two groups of eight hundreds, each comprising one quarter (or "*ferding*") of the total hidage of the shire; one group lay in the extreme south-west and the other in the extreme north-east, this latter unit representing possibly the survival of a seventh-century *regio*.[3]

The imposition of hidation upon the south-western group of eight hundreds, which never came under Scandinavian control (it lay on the English side of

[1] Some of the apparent discrepancies may arise from mistakes on my part in reconstructing the hundredal assessments, rather than from temporary alterations to the hundredal boundaries. Everyone working in this field will be acquainted with the pitfalls of Domesday statistics. A few holdings, notably Helidon and Whittlebury, are omitted altogether from the Domesday Survey, and there may be other minor sources of error.

[2] *CS* 712, a Thorney charter dated 937 but surviving only in a fourteenth-century transcript, relates to 5 hides at *Niwantun*, which can be shown from the boundary clause to be Water Newton, Hunts. There is no reason to suppose that the text is other than authentic. If Huntingdonshire was hidated at this date, we may be sure that so, too, was Northamptonshire. See further, C. Hart, *The Early Charters of Eastern England*, 1966, pp. 150–5.

[3] Cf. Bede, *Historia Ecclesiastica*, v, 19, where the monastery lying *in provincia Undalum* is presumably Peterborough (first foundation). The eight hundreds of Oundle occur in R XL, describing events before 984, and later Peterborough records enable them to be identified as the double hundreds of *Nassaburgh* and *Navereslund*, together with the four single hundreds of Huxloe, Polebrook, Navisford, and Willybrook (Cam, *op. cit.*, p. 101, n. 1).

the boundary settled by Alfred's treaty with Guthrum), could well have antedated Edward the Elder's re-conquest of the rest of the territory of Northamptonshire. In fact it is within this south-western corner, if anywhere within the county, that one would expect to find traces of the initial hidation of the Mercian era. Moreover, the assessment of these hundreds remained virtually intact right up to the time of the Norman Conquest.

Together with this 'English' group, a further unit of seven hundreds on the 'Danish' side of Watling Street also failed to secure any significant reduction in hidage assessments before the Conquest. Altogether, therefore, a total of 1,500 hides, or nearly half the county, retained its nominal hidation untouched throughout the last century and a half of the Anglo-Saxon period. This comprised all the territory lying to the west and south of Northampton town, the boundary lines between the areas of intact hidation and reduced assessment being the River Nene and its tributary the Northern Water.[1]

The Geld Roll shows that by the time of the Conquest the remainder of the county, amounting originally to 1,700 hides, had had its nominal assessment reduced by 536½ hides, or almost precisely one third, if we allow 25 hides for the borough of Northampton. The reduction was applied to groups of hundreds, and the further each group lay to the north-east (i.e. the further it lay within the Danelaw), the greater was the reduction secured in its hidation. The double hundred of *Hwicceslea* in the extreme north of the county forms the only exception to this progressive pattern of reduction, which is best illustrated in the table on p. 41 (the hundreds are represented by Roman numerals, for ease of reference to the map).

For the time of the Confessor, therefore, we obtain from the Geld Roll this picture of differential reduction in hidation as we pass north-eastwards through the county. It is clear from Table VIII that these block reductions in round figures applied to groups of hundreds must have arisen from a single administrative act at a definite point in time—they cannot represent the end result of countless acts of beneficial hidation applied to individual estates over a long period. It will be argued below that they were made after King Edmund's redemption of the Five Boroughs in 942. Whenever they were made, these new arrangements survived, with minor modifications, until the Norman Conquest.

It was this hidation which formed the basis for the dramatically unsuccessful county levy made soon after Norman rule had been established, and duly recorded in the Northants. Geld Roll. Clearly this would not do, and some master mind at the centre sent out instructions to the county officials which resulted in an administrative upheaval. The hidage of the county was to be

[1] For the Northern Water, see *VCH*, *Northants.*, I, p. 68. It was an important inter-hundredal boundary in the late Saxon period.

Table VIII: The Pre-Conquest Reduction of Hidation by Groups of Hundreds

	Basic Hundredal Hidation	*Reduced Hidation*	*Percentage Reduction*
First Group			
Nos. I–VIII and XX, each of 100h; Nos. IX–XII, each of 150h	1,500	1,500	0
Second Group			
Nos. XIII and XIV, each reduced to 90h	600	500	10
Nos. XV and XVI, each reduced to 80h			20
Nos. XVII and XVIII (double hundred), each reduced to 80h			20
Third Group*			
Nos. XXIII–XXVI, each reduced to 62h	400	248	38
Fourth Group			
No. XIX, reduced to 60h; No. XXI, reduced to 40h	200	100	50
Fifth Group			
No. XXII, reduced to 47h; No. XXVII (double hundred), reduced to 108½h	300	155½	48
Sixth Group			
Nos. XXVIII and XXIX (double hundred), each reduced to 80h	200	160	20
Totals	3,200	2,663½	—

* The reduction of this group was evidently from 400h to 250h. Shared between the four component hundreds, each would contribute 62½ hides to the new assessment. Evidently the odd half hide was ignored.

halved (from 2,663½ to 1,280) and the inequalities of assessment between the two ends of the county were to be ironed out. Henceforth each hundred was to answer for 40 hides, each 'hundred and a half' for 60 hides, and each double hundred for 80 hides.

The individual adjustments were made in the hundred courts, each adopting its own method of distributing the reductions among its constituent estates. For the south-western hundreds, each formerly assessed at 100 hides, the problem was an easy one. Every unit of five hides was reduced to two hides, whence the beautifully consistent 2h:5p ratio to be found in the tables summarizing the Domesday statistics of these hundreds.

For the remaining hundreds, the task was not so simple. Let us consider first the three 'hundreds and a half' of Nobottle Grove, Guilsborough, and Wymersley, lying between Watling Street and Northampton. These had somehow secured an interim reduction, by which each 10-hide unit had its assessment cut down, in the case of Wymersley to 9 hides, and in the case of Nobottle Grove and of Guilsborough to 8 hides. To achieve the final reduction, each Wymersley unit was now assessed at only 3½ hides, and each unit in the other two 'hundreds and a half' was halved to form a 4-hide assessment. At this distance, we cannot penetrate the mystery of the interim assessments of these hundreds, but their remarkably consistent 4h : 8p and 3½h : 9p ratios form one of the hidden wonders of the Northamptonshire Domesday, and are a sharp reminder that the members of the hundred moots were not all mere country yokels; some at least were competent and hard-headed men of business, well able to manipulate complicated sets of figures to ensure a fair distribution of the hundred's liabilities among its constituent estates.

The hundreds of Spelhoe and Hamfordshoe also achieved their new 40-hide ratings by halving the previous assessments, but for the remaining hundreds, lying to the north-eastern end of the county, we have no means of discovering just how their new rating systems were arrived at, for few records have survived of their earlier estate assessments to the geld. We find their final assessments entered in Domesday as 3-, 4-, 5-, or 10-hide units, according to the hundred concerned. Two adjacent hundreds, which probably shared a common hundred court, even adopted 4¾-hide units for the new régime (*Malesle* and Orlingbury). From evidence which is considered below, we may suppose that the initial geld assessments imposed by Edward the Elder on these north-eastern hundreds were modified by the Danish landowners to fit in with a duodecimal system of carucation.

So far in this summary we have been discussing only the *geld liability* of the assessment units for each estate. The reductions in hidation brought with them no problems in computing the amount to be paid. A levy of 2*s*. per hide would yield 7*s*. from a 3½-hide unit and 9*s*. 6*d*. from a 4¾-hide unit, calculations within the ability of the simplest type of landowner. But what of the other public liabilities falling on an estate when its hidage was reduced? Relief from the geld was one thing—flexibility is one of the essentials of any form of national taxation—but there is little scope for flexibility in assessing the obligation to repair bridges and the walls of fortresses, whose measurements stay distressingly the same; nor can one believe that reduction in the geld liability of Northamptonshire brought with it a corresponding reduction in the size of the *fyrd* to be supplied by the county in the years immediately following the Norman Conquest, before the system of knight service (which in time replaced the *fyrd*) was established.

It was necessary therefore to preserve for each estate some record of its early (post-Danish) hidation, so that its assessment for public liability (other than geld) should be known, both by its owner and also by the administrative officials of the shire and hundred courts. For Northamptonshire, the term universally adopted in Domesday Book for this liability was the ploughland—'land for X ploughs'.

THE DANISH INFLUENCE ON HIDATION

We take now a parting look at the fundamental characteristic of Northamptonshire's hidation, the differential reduction in geld assessment secured at an early date in the north-east of the county. That the amount of taxation relief obtained was directly proportional to the density of Danish settlement can be demonstrated with precision by comparing the topographical distribution of the figures in Table VIII with studies of the differential frequency of Scandinavian place-name elements from hundred to hundred. This place-name evidence establishes beyond doubt that the density of Danish settlement increased steadily towards the north-eastern tip of the county;[1] the hidage reduction follows an identical distribution pattern.

There is every reason to believe that in the north-east of the county (as also

[1] This is best brought out by the map entitled 'The Scandinavian Element' in the folder of *PN Northants*. This map is based mainly on the minor Scandinavian place-names, the significance of which as an index of settlement was explained by F. M. Stenton in 1942 (*Trans. R. Hist. Soc.*, XXIV, pp. 4–8). A later map produced by the English Place-Name Society seeks to illustrate the density of Scandinavian settlement from the distribution of parish names thought to be of Scandinavian origin, including those ending in *-by* (*English Place-Name Elements*, ed. A. H. Smith, 2 vols., 1956, map no. 10; the map is reproduced by P. H. Sawyer, *The Age of the Vikings*, 1962, p. 157; see also the map of 'place-names in *-by* existing in 1086', on p. 133 of F. T. Wainwright's *Archaeology, Place-Names, and History*, 1962). The element *-by* is however a dangerous one to use as an index of Scandinavian settlement, for many Domesday place-names ending in *-bi* may have originated from OE *byrig*. The case of Badby in Northamptonshire is an important example; the DB spelling is *Badebi* but in *CS* 792, an original charter dated 944, the spellings are *Baddanbyrig*, *Baddanbyrg*, and *Baddanby*; the first element is clearly OE *Badda*. The name was evidently Scandinavianized some time between 944 and 1086, and is therefore not available as evidence of early Danish settlement. This process of Scandinavianization went on over a long period of time, as evidenced by the development of the Northamptonshire village names Thornby, Naseby, and Kirby Hall (in Gretton). The DB forms are *Torneberie*, *Navesberie*, and *Chercheberi*, but in all three cases the second element (clearly originally OE *byrig*) developed into *-bi* some time after 1086 (note that in all three cases the first elements are of OE origin). For this reason, I am convinced that Northamptonshire villages with DB names ending in *-bi* or *-by* cannot be used to illustrate the density of Scandinavian settlement in the county, unless they have first elements of certain Danish origin. The only names within this category would appear to be those of Catesby and Holdenby; even here, one must remember that Scandinavian personal names such as Kati and Halfdan were given to Englishmen before the Norman Conquest. See further, *PN Northants.*, pp. xxi–xxiii; Sawyer, *op. cit.*, pp. 152–63; Wainwright, *op. cit.*, pp. 73–84.

in large parts of Cambridgeshire) the Danish landowners were left virtually unmolested when King Edward the Elder re-conquered the territory which became Northamptonshire.[1] He allowed them to meet their public liabilities (other than geld) according to their own Danish assessment pattern;[2] but the geld itself had to be raised by a uniform system throughout the country, and for this reason alone a hidage assessment was imposed on the Danish landowners. At some stage this imposition was successfully challenged, and a substantial reduction was obtained.

We have then to ask ourselves when, and by whom, this geld reduction was achieved. The adjacent hundreds of Huntingdonshire, which had been almost completely cleared of their Danish landowners when re-conquered by Edward the Elder, received (like the south-western hundreds of Northamptonshire, which the Danes never penetrated) no hidage reduction at all. The Northamptonshire reductions, it would seem, were made to benefit Danish land owners.

By the time of Bishop Æthelwold's death in 984, the great fenland abbey which he had re-founded at Peterborough possessed almost every estate situated in the double hundred of Nassaburgh, which in later ages became the Soke of Peterborough.[3] The fact that its hidation TRE as recorded in the Geld Roll does not differ in nature from those of the rest of the north-eastern hundreds of Northamptonshire, argues very strongly that this double hundred received its reduction in assessment (which was less than those obtained for the hundreds of *Stoche* and Corby) before Æthelwold had purchased its constituent estates from the Danish landholders. The duodecimal character of the hidation of the individual estates which he bought also shows that the reduction had already been accomplished by this time; what settles the argument is the existence, in the document recording Æthelwold's purchases, of the oxgang as a subdivision of the 'hide' at Wittering, for the oxgang is a unit met with elsewhere only in the Danelaw; the name 'hide' must here have been applied to what was in fact the Danelaw carucate. The bulk of Æthelwold's purchases were made very soon after his re-foundation of Peterborough Abbey in 963. The outside dates for the reduction in hidation in north-eastern Northamptonshire may therefore safely be given as 917 and 963.[4]

[1] The evidence for this statement will be fully displayed in my forthcoming book entitled *The Hide in English History*. At this stage I will merely refer to the *Liber Eliensis*, which suggests that the Danes of Huntingdonshire were dispossessed, but that those of Cambridgeshire were left on their estates (*Liber Eliensis*, ed. E. O. Blake, Royal Historical Society, Camden series, XCII, 1962, pp. xi, 98–9).

[2] It is becoming increasingly clear that after Alfred's treaty with Guthrum, the Danes replaced the English hidation of the districts in which they settled by a system of assessment that was entirely their own. On this, see C. F. Slade, *The Leicestershire Survey*, 1956, p. 77, and C. Hart, 'The Hidation of Huntingdonshire', in *Proceedings of the Cambridge Antiquarian Society*, LXI, 1968, pp. 55–66.

[3] R XL, and other early Peterborough Charters.

[4] For the earlier of these two dates, see footnote 4, page 14.

In all the period between the conquest of Northamptonshire by Edward the Elder and the re-foundation of Peterborough Abbey by Bishop Æthelwold we know of one occasion, and one only, when the local Danish landowners could have been in a position to persuade the monarchy to grant them *en bloc* so large and permanent a beneficial assessment: the months immediately following King Edmund's redemption of the Five Boroughs in 942.[1] At no other time does the English monarchy appear to have been nearly so dependent on the goodwill of its Danish subjects in the neighbourhood.

The following summary will perhaps assist readers to follow the argument which has now been developed:

Table IX: Stages in the Pattern of Hidation in Northamptonshire

Phase I:	The Initial or Tribal Hidation, lasting from the sixth or seventh century to 887.
Phase II:	The Carucation imposed in 887 by the earl of the Danish army based on Northampton. This Carucation completely replaced the Hidation of Phase I, and lasted from 887 to *c.* 917.
Phase III:	The Second Hidation, imposed by Edward the Elder, lasting from *c.* 917 to 942. This replaced the Carucation of Phase II for purposes of taxation only; the Carucation was preserved until 1086 for the assessment of other public burdens.
Phase IV:	The pattern following the 'Danish' reduction in hidation, lasting from 942 to *c.* 1067.
Phase V:	The pattern following the 'Norman' reduction in hidation, lasting from *c.* 1067 to the mid-twelfth century or later.

THE COUNTY HIDAGE—A POSTSCRIPT

It will readily be appreciated that if the foregoing thesis is accepted, then we are faced with an entirely new interpretation of the County Hidage. This document in its original form cannot be dated later than 942, for it assigns 3,200 hides to Northamptonshire, which was the figure before any reduction took place. The County Hidage, then, records a new schedule of assessment imposed throughout the Midlands by Edward the Elder. It is contemporary with, and complementary to, the Burghal Hidage, a document which deals with the military organization of the more stable parts of Edward's kingdom. And as has already been pointed out, it establishes the line of cleavage between the

[1] F. M. Stenton, *Anglo-Saxon England*, 2nd edn, 1947, p. 354. Since I wrote this, a detailed examination of the Cambridgeshire hidation has led me to a similar conclusion concerning the date of the hidage reduction of that shire. I hope to publish this in due course.

hidated shires, and the carucated shires of the Northern Danelaw. Northamptonshire was a border county, in many respects the most Scandinavianized of the hidated shires, and it is to this circumstance that it owes its highly complicated and elaborately recorded pattern of assessment.

APPENDIX

THE HUNDREDAL ASSESSMENTS OF THE NORTHAMPTONSHIRE DOMESDAY

Abbreviations

h = hide
p = ploughland
bov = bovate
v = virgate
a = (geld) acre

Roman numerals allocated to individual hundreds are those appearing on the accompanying map. On the map the names of certain hundreds are underlined, and in the text and Appendix printed in italic; these names did not survive as hundred names after the early medieval period. The individual holdings are listed according to their Domesday tenant-in-chief, to facilitate their identification with the appropriate DB entries. Place-names of holdings which are unlocated appear in italic. Where holdings are grouped together for purposes of illustrating the assessment, they are usually adjacent to each other topographically.

It is clear from many entries that the equations 1h = 4v = 120a and 2bov = 1v apply to the DB geld units of this county. Occasionally fractions of ploughlands are expressed according to the equation 8 oxen = 1p.

For reasons explained in *VCH, Northants.*, I, pp. 269–71, entries relating to certain holdings in Warwickshire, Staffordshire, and Oxfordshire are included in the Northamptonshire portion of the Domesday Survey. These have been omitted from the tables which follow. Entries relating to Farndish and Puddington (on the Bedfordshire/Northamptonshire border) and to Stibbington, Elton, Thurning, and Catworth (on the Huntingdonshire/Northamptonshire border) have, however, been included within the tables for their adjacent Northamptonshire hundreds, as there is reason to believe that they formed part of the assessment for these hundreds.

I King's Sutton

Domesday Tenant-in-Chief	*Holding*	*Hides*		*Ploughlands*		
Robert de Oilgi	Purston in King's Sutton	$\frac{1}{2}$h+$\frac{1}{5}$h	2h	1$\frac{1}{2}$p	2$\frac{1}{2}$p	5p
Count of Mortain	Purston in King's Sutton	$\frac{1}{2}$h		1p		
King's Almsmen	King's Sutton	3v+$\frac{1}{5}$v		2p	2$\frac{1}{2}$p	
Count of Mortain	King's Sutton	$\frac{1}{5}$h		$\frac{1}{2}$p		
Hugh de Grenmaisnil	King's Sutton	1$\frac{1}{2}$h+$\frac{1}{10}$h		4p	10p	
King	King's Sutton	3h		6p		
King	Walton Grounds in King's Sutton	1v +$\frac{1}{5}$v		1p	3p	15p
Count of Mortain	Walton Grounds in King's Sutton	$\frac{1}{2}$h		1p		
Count of Mortain	Walton Grounds in King's Sutton	1h+1 bov		1p		
Gunfrid de Cioches	Grimsbury in Warksworth	2h+($\frac{1}{5}\times 2$)h		6p		
Count of Mortain	Charlton in Newbottle	1$\frac{1}{2}$h		3$\frac{1}{2}$p	6p	
Ghilo brother of Anculf	Land belonging to Steane	$\frac{4}{5}$h		2p		
Bishop of Coutances	Croughton	($\frac{4}{5}\times\frac{1}{2}$)h		$\frac{1}{2}$p		
Count of Mortain	Middleton Cheney	2h	4h	5p	10p	
Hugh de Grenmaisnil	Middleton Cheney	2h		5p		
Earl Hugh of Chester	Middleton Cheney	($\frac{4}{5}\times 2$)h		4p	10p	
Manno	Thenford	1h	2h	2$\frac{1}{2}$p		
Robert de Oilgi	Thenford	1h		3$\frac{1}{2}$p		
Earl Aubrey of Northumbria	Farthinghoe	4h		10p		
Walter the Fleming	Astwick in Evenley	1$\frac{1}{2}$h+($\frac{1}{5}\times\frac{1}{2}$)h	2h	4p	5p	10p
Count of Mortain	Croughton (berewick in Evenley)	($\frac{4}{5}\times\frac{1}{2}$)h		1p		
Earl Aubrey of Northumbria	Evenley	3v	2h−$\frac{1}{3}$v	2p	5p	
Geoffrey de Mandeville	Croughton	1h+$\frac{2}{3}$v		3p		
Hugh de Grenmaisnil	Newbottle	6h		15p		
King	Charlton in Newbottle	3v+$\frac{1}{5}$v	4h	2p	10p	
Geoffrey de Mandeville	Aynho	3h+$\frac{1}{5}$h		8p		
Geoffrey de Mandeville	Croughton	($\frac{1}{2}\times\frac{1}{5}$)h		$\frac{1}{4}$p		
	Totals	39h+9a		95$\frac{1}{4}$p		

II *Eadboldestowe*

Domesday Tenant-in-Chief	*Holding*	*Hides*		*Ploughlands*		
Earl Aubrey of Northumbria	Brackley	2h		5p		
Earl Hugh of Chester	Radstone	2h		5p		
Walter the Fleming	Evenley	2h		5p		
Ghilo brother of Anculf	Steane	2h		5p		
Ghilo brother of Anculf	Thorpe Mandeville	2h		5p		
Ghilo brother of Anculf	Stuchbury	2h		5p		
Ghilo brother of Anculf	Astwell	2h		5p		
Bishop of Lincoln	Chalcombe	4h		10p		
Count of Mortain	Helmdon	4h		10p		
Earl Hugh of Chester	Marsdon St Lawrence	4h		10p		
Earl Aubrey of Northumbria	Halse in Brackley	2h	6h		12½p	15p
Earl Aubrey of Northumbria	Syresham	2h				
Earl Aubrey of Northumbria	Brackley	1h				
Count of Mortain	Evenley	1h		2½p		
Count of Mortain	Syresham	½h	1h	1¼p	2½p	
Ghilo brother of Anculf	Syresham	½h		1¼p		
Earl Aubrey of Northumbria	Syresham	⅔h		—		
Geoffrey de Mandeville	Culworth	1½h+⅔v	4h+8a	4p	10p	
Ghilo brother of Anculf	*Brime* in Culworth	2h+(⅘×½)h		6p		
King	Whitfield	2h		*inland* for 2p		
				for the men 5p		
	Totals	39h+88a		99½p		

III Chipping Warden

Domesday Tenant-in-Chief	*Holding*	*Hides*		*Ploughlands*	
Bishop of Bayeux	Greatworth	2h		5p	
Bishop of Coutances	Edgecote	2h		5p	
Count of Mortain	Boddington	2h		5p	
Hugh de Grenmaisnil	Byfield	2h		5p	
Hugh de Grenmaisnil	Woodford	2h		5p	
Hugh de Grenmaisnil	Eydon	2h		5p	
Geoffrey de Mandeville	Hinton in Woodford	2h		5p	
Ghilo brother of Anculf	Sulgrave	4h		10p	
Earl Hugh of Chester	Byfield	8h		20p	
Count of Mortain	West Farndon in Woodford	1½h+1 bov	2h	2p	3p
Hugh de Grenmaisnil	Farndon	1½v		1p	
Guy de Reinbuedcurt	Chipping Warden	2h 3v	4h	6½p	9p
Earl Hugh of Chester	Trafford House in Chipping Warden	1h 1v		2½p	
Geoffrey de Mandeville	Ashton le Walls	6h		10p	
Earl Hugh of Chester	Boddington	1h		2½p	
Robert of Stadford	*Stantone*	3v		3p	
	Totals	39h 3v		92½p	

IV Green's Norton (*Foxle*)

Domesday Tenant-in-Chief	*Holding*	*Hides*			*Ploughlands*		
Count of Mortain	Blakesley	$1\frac{1}{2}$h	2h		$3\frac{1}{2}$p	5p	
Earl Hugh of Chester	Blakesley	$\frac{1}{2}$h		4h	$1\frac{1}{2}$p		10p
William Peverell	Blakesley	2h			5p		
King	Green's Norton						
King	Adstone	7h+1v	$7\frac{1}{2}$h		—		
King	Adstone						
King's Almsmen	Adstone	1v			$\frac{1}{2}$p		
Robert de Todeni	Seawell farm in Blakesley	3h+$\frac{4}{5}$v		12h	7p		$10\frac{1}{2}$p
Count of Mortain	Adstone	1v+$\frac{1}{5}$v	$3\frac{1}{2}$h		1p		
Ghilo brother of Anculf	Silverstone	$\frac{1}{2}$h	1h		1p		
Geoffrey de Mandeville	Silverstone	$\frac{1}{2}$h			1p		
Earl Hugh of Chester	Slapton	4h			10p		
Walter the Fleming	Canon's Ashby	$2\frac{1}{2}$h	4h		6p		12p
Ghilo brother of Anculf	Moreton Pinkney	$1\frac{1}{2}$h			6p		
Walter the Fleming	Plumpton	1h	4h		4p		$11\frac{1}{2}$p
Ghilo brother of Anculf	Weedon Lois	3h			$7\frac{1}{2}$p		
David	Bradden	1h+$(\frac{4}{5}\times\frac{1}{2})$h	$2\frac{4}{5}$h		$3\frac{1}{2}$p	7p	
Robert de Buci	Bradden	1h+$(\frac{4}{5}\times\frac{1}{2})$h		5h	$3\frac{1}{2}$p		12p
Hugh de Grenmaisnil	Maidford	$2\frac{1}{5}$h			5p		
	Totals	33h			66p		

V Cleyley

Domesday Tenant-in-Chief	*Holding*	*Hides*			*Ploughlands*	
Manno	Wicken	3v	2h		3p	13p
Robert de Oilgi	Wicken	1h+1v			10p	
King	Passenham	1h		4h	12p	
King's Almsmen	Passenham	½h	2h		—	13p
King	Puxley in Passenham	½h			1p	
Bishop of Bayeux	Puxley in Passenham	½h−(⅕×½)h			1p	
Countess Judith	Potterspury	1h×⅕h		8h	3p	22p
Henry de Ferriers	Potterspury	3h+⅕h			10p	
Walter the Fleming	*unnamed*	3h+⅕h			8p	
Count Alan of Brittany	Wakefield Lawn in Potterspury	(⅘×½)h		4h	8p	17p
William Peverell	Paulerspury	3½h+(⅕×½)h			9p	
Count of Mortain	Furtho	2h			6p	
Count of Mortain	Furtho	$\frac{9}{10}$h			2p	
Count of Mortain	Furtho	½h+(⅘×½)h			3½p	
Count of Mortain	Cosgrove	(⅘×½)h		4h−2a	1p	9½p
William Peverell	*Aceshille*	½h−⅕h			—	
Winemar	Cosgrove	½h−(⅕×1)v			1½p	
Count of Mortain	Cosgrove	⅚h			1½p	
Gunfrid de Cioches	Hulcote in Easton Neston	3v+¼v	6½v		2p	
Gunfrid de Cioches	Easton Neston	3v+¼v			2p	
Winemar	Easton Neston	2½v		6h	1p	21p
Count of Mortain	Easton Neston	1h+2½v			6p	
Count of Mortain	Alderton	2h+½v			8p	
Count of Mortain	Alderton	1h			2p	
Suain	Stoke Bruerne	4h			10p	
Bishop of Bayeux	Roade	1h			—	
Gunfrid de Cioches	Roade	(⅘×½)h	2h+3a		1p	
*William Peverell	Courteenhall	½h+½v		4h+3a	1p	7p
Count of Mortain	Grafton Regis	⅘h	2h		2p	
Winemar	Ashton	1h+(⅘×1)v			3p	
Winemar	Ashton	(⅘×½)h		5h	1p	11p
Bishop of Bayeux	Hartwell	4½h+(⅕×½)h			10p	
	Totals	41h+1a			129½p	

* Cf. J. H. Round, *VCH, Northants.*, I, p. 374, n. 14.

VI Towcester

Domesday Tenant-in-Chief	*Holding*	*Hides*			*Ploughlands*
Geoffrey de Mandeville	Hinton-in-the-Hedges	2h			5p
Walter the Fleming	Evenley	4h			10p
Ghilo brother of Anculf	Wappenham	2h			5p
Walter de Aincurt	Pattishall	8h			20p
Walter de Aincurt	Ascote in Pattishall	2h			5p
Walter de Aincurt	Grimscote in Cold Higham	2h			5p
Count of Mortain	Foxley	$(\frac{4}{5}\times\frac{1}{2})$h	} $2\frac{4}{5}$h		1p
Count of Mortain	Cold Higham	2h+$(\frac{4}{5}\times\frac{1}{2})$h	}		6p
Sigar de Cioches	Gayton	4h+$(\frac{4}{5}\times\frac{1}{2})$h			10p
Count of Mortain	Tiffield	$1\frac{1}{2}$h+$\frac{1}{5}$h	} $2\frac{2}{5}$h	} 3h	4p
Count of Mortain	Tiffield	$\frac{1}{2}$h+$\frac{1}{5}$h	}	}	$1\frac{1}{2}$p
King's Sokemen	Towcester	$\frac{1}{2}$h+$(\frac{1}{5}\times\frac{1}{2})$h		}	—
King	Towcester	$7\frac{1}{2}$h			22p
	Totals	37h+84a			$94\frac{1}{2}$p

VII Fawsley (*Gravesende*)

Domesday Tenant-in-Chief	*Holding*	*Hides*				*Ploughlands*		
*[Count of Mortain	Helidon	4h				—]		
Gilbert de Gand	Stowe Nine Churches	4h				10p		
Evesham Abbey	Litchborough	4h				10p		
Count of Mortain	*Chelverdescote* (=Newnham)	4h				10p		
William Peverell	Catesby	4h				8p		
King's Almsmen	Fawsley	$(\frac{4}{5}\times\frac{1}{2})$h		2h		1p	5p	
Walter the Fleming	*unnamed*	$1\frac{1}{2}$h$+(\frac{1}{5}\times\frac{1}{2})$h				4p		
Count of Mortain	Charwelton	$\frac{1}{2}$h	1h			1p		
Thorney Abbey	Charwelton	$\frac{1}{2}$h			4h	1p		10p
Bishop of Bayeux	Everdon	$\frac{1}{2}$h		2h		1p	5p	
Count of Mortain	Snorscomb in Everdon	$\frac{1}{2}$v	1h			1p		
Count of Mortain	Snorscomb in Everdon	$1\frac{1}{2}$v				1p		
Count of Mortain	Little Preston	1h$+\frac{1}{2}$v		$1\frac{1}{2}$h		3p		
Count of Mortain	Little Preston	$1\frac{1}{2}$v			4h	1p		11p
King	Fawsley	$1\frac{1}{2}$h$+\frac{1}{5}$h		$2\frac{1}{2}$h		4p†		
Count of Mortain	Preston Capes	$\frac{4}{5}$h				3p		
Count of Mortain	Farthingstone	3h+1v		3h$+1\frac{1}{2}$v		8p	9p	
Count of Mortain	Farthingstone	$\frac{1}{2}$v			7h$+\frac{1}{2}$v	1p		18p
Hugh de Grenmaisnil	Weedon Beck	$3\frac{1}{2}$h		$3\frac{1}{2}$h+1v		$8\frac{1}{2}$p	9p	
Hugh de Grenmaisnil	Charwelton	1v				$\frac{1}{2}$p		
	Totals	35h+15a				77p‡		

* Holding omitted from DB; details supplied from Northants. Survey. † "*Inland* for 4p".

‡ If we add 10p for Helidon, the total is 87p.

VIII *Egelweardesle*

Domesday Tenant-in-Chief	*Holding*	*Hides*				*Ploughlands*		
Coventry Abbey	Kilsby	2h				5p		
Crowland Abbey	Badby	4h				10p		
Hugh de Grenmaisnil	Ashby St Ledgers	4h				10p		
William Peverell	Barby	2h	4h			5p	10p	
William Peverell	Barby	2h				5p		
Countess Judith	Daventry	8h				16p		
Countess Judith	Welton & Thrupp Grounds	½h + 1v − (⅕ × ½)h	3h + 1v			1p		
Count of Meulan	Norton	2½h + (⅕ × ½)h		4h		7p	10½p	
Count of Mortain	Thrupp Grounds	⅔h	3v			2p		
Count of Mortain	Welton	½v − 5a			8h	½p		19½p
Gunfrid de Cioches	Thrupp Grounds	½h + (⅕ × ½)h	1h			1p		
Hugh de Grenmaisnil	Thrupp Grounds	(⅘ × ½)h		4h		1p	9p	
Count of Mortain	Dodford	3h				7p		
Hugh de Grenmaisnil	Staverton	1h				2½p		
Hugh de Grenmaisnil	Welton	3h − 1v	4h			7p	19½p	
Bishop of Bayeux	Braunston	1v		7½h		1p		
Walter de Aincurt	Braunston	3½h				9p		
	Totals	37½h				90p		

IX Guilsborough (1½ hundreds)

Domesday Tenant-in-Chief	Holding	Hides			Ploughlands	
William Peverell	Winwick	3v	4h		1p	7½p
Coventry Abbey	Winwick	3h + 1v			6½p	
Gilbert	Watford	2h	4h		4p	8p
Coventry Abbey	West Haddon	2h			4p	
William Peverell	West Haddon	1½v			1p	
Gunfrid de Cioches	West Haddon	1v	4h + ½v		½p	8½p
Gunfrid de Cioches	Long Buckby	2½h + 1v			5½p	
Count of Mortain	Long Buckby	3v			1½p	
Count of Mortain	Nortoft Grange in Guilsborough	2h			4p	
William Peverell	Guilsborough	3½v			1½p	
William Peverell	Cotton under Guilsborough	3½v	4h		3p	8½p
Count of Mortain	Guilsborough	1v			'waste'	
William Peverell	Nortoft Grange in Guilsborough	½h			1p	
Count of Mortain	Little Creaton	½h			1p	
Robert de Buci	Great Creaton	1v	1h + 3v		2 oxen (= ¼p)	
Gunfrid de Cioches	Great Creaton	1h			2p	
Bishop of Lincoln	Hollowell	1h + (⅔ × ½)h		4h + ⅔v	3p	8⅛p
Gilbert	Hollowell	⅔v			⅜p	
Count of Mortain	Hollowell	⅓v	1h + 3⅔v		'waste'	
Count of Mortain	Hollowell	⅓v			'waste'	
William Peverell	Hollowell	1v			½p	
Walter the Fleming	Cottesbrooke	1h + 1v	1h + 3v		2½p	
William	Cottesbrooke	½h			1p	
William Peverell	Thornby	1h	1h + 2v		2p	
William Peverell	Thornby	½h		4h	½p	7½p
Count of Mortain	Chilcote's Cover in Cold Ashby	1v	3v		½p	
Count of Mortain	Cold Ashby	½h			1p	
Count of Mortain	Cold Ashby	1½h	4h		3p	8p
Coventry Abbey	Cold Ashby	2½h			5p	
William Peverell	Cold Ashby	1½v	1h		1p	
Geoffrey de Wirce	Cold Ashby	2½v		8h	1p	16p
William Peverell	Naseby	7h			14p	
Geoffrey de Wirce	Welford	4h			8p	

IX Guilsborough (1½ hundreds)—continued

Domesday Tenant-in-Chief	*Holding*	*Hides*			*Ploughlands*	
Count of Mortain	Elkington	1h + 3v	2h	4h − ½v	3½p	8⅞p
Guy de Reinbuedcurt	Elkington	¾v			3 oxen (= ⅜p)	
Geoffrey de Wirce	Elkington	¼v			—	
Guy de Reinbuedcurt	Stanford	2h − ½v			5p	
Earl Aubrey of Northumbria	Lilbourne	2h + ½v	4h		4¼p	7½p
Earl Aubrey of Northumbria	Lilbourne	1½v			¾p	
Count of Mortain	Yelvertoft	3v			1p	
Count of Mortain	Yelvertoft	3v			1½p	
Count of Mortain	Lilbourne	1v	4h		2½p	10½p
Geoffrey de Wirce	Crick	4h − 1v			8p	
Earl Hugh of Chester	Yelvertoft	2h + 1v			4p	
	Totals	54h + 50a			111p	

X Nobottle Grove (1½ hundreds)

Domesday Tenant-in-Chief	*Holding*	*Hides*					*Ploughlands*		
Count of Mortain	Bugbrook	4h					10p		
Count of Mortain	Kislingbury	½h	4h				1p	11p	
Gilbert de Gand	Kislingbury	3½h					10p		
William Peverell	Duston	4h					8p		
Peterborough Knights	Dallington	4h					8p		
Count of Mortain	Brampton	4h − 5a					8p		
Count of Mortain	Brampton	½h	4h + 7½a				1p	9¼p	
Count of Mortain	Harleston	½ bov					¼p		
Count of Mortain	Harleston	1½h					3p		
William Peverell	Harleston	1½h					3p		
King	Harleston	½h					2p		
Count of Mortain	Holdenby	2h + 1v	4h				8p	12p	
Count of Mortain	Holdenby	1h + 3v					4p		
William Peverell	Teeton	2h		4h			4p	9½p	
Count of Mortain	Ravensthorpe	½h	2h				2p		
William Peverell	Ravensthorpe	1h + 1v					3p		
Gilbert	Ravensthorpe	1v					½p		
Count of Mortain	East Haddon	2½h	4h				5p	8p	
Count of Mortain	East Haddon	1½h					3p		
Count of Mortain	East Haddon	½h	1h + 3v		4h		1p	12p	
Count of Mortain	Great Brington	½h					3p		
Count of Mortain	Brockhall, and Muscot in Norton	3v					2p		
Count of Mortain	Althorp	⅔h	1h + ½v	2h + 1v			2p		
William Peverell	Althorp	⅓h + ½v					1p		
William Peverell	Nobottle in Brington	1h + ½v					3p		
William Peverell	Great Brington	1½h	4h	6h		12h	2p	8p	18p
William Peverell	Harpole	2½h					6p		
King	Upton	2h					10p		
Count of Mortain	Whilton	1h			6h		2p	11p	
Bishop of Bayeux	Lower Heyford	2h + 1½v	3h + 3v	5h			4p		
Gilbert de Gand	Lower Heyford	1h + 1½v					2p		
William Peverell	Glassthorpehill in Floore	½v	1h + 1v				—		
Count of Mortain	Glassthorpehill in Floore	3v					3p		
Geoffrey de Mandeville	Floore	½h	2h	4h			1p	10p	
William Peverell	Floore	½h					1p		
William de Cahainges	Floore	1h					3p		
Gunfrid de Cioches	Floore	1h + 1v	2h				3p		
Count of Mortain	Floore	3v					2p		

X Nobottle Grove ($1\frac{1}{2}$ hundreds)—continued

Domesday Tenant-in-Chief	*Holding*	*Hides*			*Ploughlands*	
Count of Mortain	Lower Heyford	$1\frac{2}{3}$v	$3\frac{1}{3}$v	1h + $1\frac{5}{12}$v	1p	3p
Count of Mortain	Lower Heyford	$1\frac{2}{3}$v			1p	
Count of Mortain	Upper Heyford	$\frac{1}{3}$v			—	
Count of Mortain	Upper Heyford	$1\frac{3}{4}$v			1p	
	Totals	57h + 50a			$137\frac{3}{4}$p	

XI Wymersley (1½ hundreds)

Domesday Tenant-in-Chief	*Holding*	*Hides*			*Ploughlands*			
Countess Judith	Yardley Hastings	3½h			9p			
Geoffrey Alselin	Milton	3½h			9p			
William Peverell	Courteenhall	3½h			9p			
William Peverell	Blisworth	3½h			9p			
Countess Judith	Grendon	3h + 1v	3½h		9p	9p		
Countess Judith	Grendon	1v			—			
Geoffrey Alselin	Rothersthorpe	½h	3½h		1p	9p		
Geoffrey Alselin	Rothersthorpe	½h			1p			
Gunfrid de Cioches	Rothersthorpe	2½h			7p			
William Peverell	Houghton	1h + ½v + 2 car	* 3½h		4p	9p		
Countess Judith	Houghton	1v			†			
Countess Judith	Houghton	2h			5p			
Ramsey Abbey	Whiston & Denton	3h	3½h		6p	9p		17½p +
Countess Judith	Denton	½h			½p			
Countess Judith	Denton	1h	1¾h	3½h	2p			
Countess Judith	Whiston	1v			½p			
Bishop of Bayeux	Houghton	1½v			4p	4p +	8½p +	
Countess Judith	Houghton	½v			—			
Bishop of Bayeux	Brafield	3v	1¾h		2p	4½p		
Countess Judith	Brafield	3v			2p			
Countess Judith	Brafield	1v			½p			
Walter the Fleming	Wooton	2½h	3½h		7p	7p +		18p +
Countess Judith	Wooton	1h			†			
Bishop of Coutances	Preston Deanery	1h	1¾h	3½h	2p	6p +		
Countess Judith	Preston Deanery	3v			†			
Geoffrey Alselin	Collingtree	2h − 1v	1¾h		4p			
Countess Judith	Quinton	½h	1¾h	3½h	1p	5p +		
Countess Judith	Quinton	3v			†			
Countess Judith	Quinton	½h			†			
Countess Judith	Piddington	1h + 3v	1¾h		4p			
Countess Judith	Castle Ashby	2h − 1v	3½h		5p	10p		18p
Drogo de Beurere	Chadstone in Castle Ashby	1h + 3v			5p			
King	Hardingstone	5h	7h		4p‡	8p		
Countess Judith	Hardingstone	2h			4p			

XI Wymersley (1½ hundreds)—continued

Domesday Tenant-in-Chief	*Holding*	*Hides*			*Ploughlands*		
Bishop of Coutances	Hackleton	½h	2½h	7h	1p	7p	13½p
Countess Judith	Hackleton	2h			6p		
Bishop of Coutances	Horton	3v	4½h		1p	6½p	
Walter the Fleming	Horton	2h			4p		
Countess Judith	Horton	1h + 1v			½p		
Countess Judith	Horton	½h			1p		
Countess Judith	Yardley Hastings Woodland	3½h			—		
Countess Judith	Little Houghton	1v	1h + 3½v		†	3½p	
Guy de Reinbuedcurt	Cogenhoe	3½v			3p		
Countess Judith	Cogenhoe	3v			½p		
	Totals	64h + 105a			133½p		

* The only reference to carucates in the Northants. section of Domesday. Apparently 2 carucates = ½ virgate.

† These holdings are all sokeland of Yardley Hastings, owned by Countess Judith. They are assessed together in Domesday as follows:

Houghton	1v	3½h assessed together as 6p.
Preston Deanery	3v	
Quinton	3v	
Quinton	½h	
Wooton	1h	
Houghton	1v	

‡ "5h, and besides the *inland* there is land for 4p."

XII Higham Ferrers (1½ hundreds)

Domesday Tenant-in-Chief	*Holding*	*Hides*				*Ploughlands*
Countess Judith	Easton Maduit	1v				½p
William Peverell	Easton Maduit	1½v				—
Countess Judith	Bozeat	1v	3h			—
William Peverell	Bozeat	1½v				½p
Countess Judith	Bozeat	2h − 1v				4p
Countess Judith	Wollaston	2h	3h			3½p
Countess Judith	Wollaston	1h				—
Gunfrid de Cioches	Wollaston	5h				10p
Count of Mortain	Irchester	2½v	2h			½p
William Peverell	Kingston in Irchester	1h + 1½v		10½h	21h	2p
Gunfrid de Cioches	Kingston in Irchester	1h + 3v	3½h			2p
William Peverell	Irchester	1h + 3v				2p
King	Part of Finedon	10½h				(21p)*
William Peverell	Rushden	6h				12p
William Peverell	Higham Ferrers	6h				12½p
Peterborough Abbey	Stanwick	1h + 1v	3h			3p
William Peverell	Chelveston & Caldecote	1h + 3v				3p
Bishop of Coutances	Raunds	6h + 1½v				—
William Peverell	Raunds	7½h + ½v	15h			14p
William Peverell	Hargrave	½h				1p
William Peverell	Poddington	½h				—
Bishop of Coutances	Denford	5h				—
Bishop of Coutances	Newton Bromswold	2h − ½v	7½h − ½v			2p
William Peverell	Farndish	½h				1p
	Totals	64h + 45ac				94½p

* Estimated share of total ploughlands alloted to Finedon.

XIII Hamfordshoe

Domesday Tenant-in-Chief	*Holding*	*Hides*	*Ploughlands*
Count of Mortain	Sywell	4h	10p
Henry de Ferriers	Ecton	4h	8p
Countess Judith	Earls Barton	4h	8p
Countess Judith	Great Doddington	4h	8p
Countess Judith	Wilby	4h	7p
Countess Judith	Mears Ashby	4h	7p
Countess Judith	Holcot	1h + 1½v } 4h	2p } 12p
King	Holcot	2h + 2½v }	10p }
Countess Judith	Holcot	½h } 1h } 2h	1p } 2p } 4p
Countess Judith	*Waleton*	½h }	1p }
Countess Judith	Hardwick	1h }	2p }
Countess Judith	Wellingborough	½h } 6h	1½p } 13½p
Crowland Abbey	Wellingborough	5½h }	12p }
Countess Judith	Wellingborough	½v	1 ox (=⅛p) } ⅝p
Bishop of Coutances	Wellingborough	1v	½p }
	Totals	36h + 45a	78⅛p

XIV Spelhoe

Domesday Tenant-in-Chief	*Holding*	*Hides*			*Ploughlands*	
Gilbert	Great Billing	4h			8p	
Richard	Abington	4h			8p	
King	Moulton	1½h + 1 bov	4h		(3p)*	8p
Robert de Buci	Moulton	2h + 1½v			5p	
Countess Judith	Moulton	3h + 1v	4h		6½p	7½p
Countess Judith	Moulton Park	½h			1p	
Countess Judith	Moulton Park	1v			—	
Countess Judith	Boughton	3h − ½v	3h	4h	6p	8p
Countess Judith	Boughton	½v			—	
Countess Judith	Boughton	3v	1h		1½p	
Countess Judith	Boughton	1v			½p	
King's Almsmen	Boughton	1½v	1h	4½h	—	9p
Robert de Buci	Boughton	3v − 1 bov			1½p	
Walter the Fleming	Pitsford	3h + 1v	3½h		7p	
Count of Mortain	Pitsford	1v			½p	
Robert de Buci	Spratton	1v + 1 bov	4h + 1 bov		½p	8½p
Count of Mortain	Spratton	3h − 1v			6p	
Countess Judith	Spratton	1h			2p	
†Count of Mortain	Little Billing	2½v	4h		1p	8p
Gunfrid de Cioches	Little Billing	3h + 1½v			7p	
King	Weston Favell	1h	4h		(2p)*	8p
Count of Mortain	Weston Favell	3h			6p	
Count of Mortain	Weston Favell	2½h	4h		5p	8p
‡St Mary of Grestain	Weston Favell	1½h			3p	
Gunfrid de Cioches	Weston Favell	½v	2h		—	5½p
Bishop of Coutances	*Hantone*§	1h + ½v			4p	
Winemar	*Hantone*§	3v			1½p	
King	Kingsthorpe	4h + 3v			20p	
	Totals	47h + 45a			106½p	

* Assessed together at 5p.

† DB has two entries for this holding. The hidation of the Northants. Survey suggests they are duplicates.

‡ This DB holding of *Westone* must be Weston Favell, and not Weston by Welland (which is nearer to the rest of St Mary's holdings), because of the hidage patterns of the respective hundreds.

§ This is, I think, Northampton.

XV *Malesle*

Domesday Tenant-in-Chief	*Holding*	*Hides*		*Ploughlands*
King	Brixworth	9½h		35p
Bury St Edmunds Abbey	Hanging Houghton	1h + ½v		3p
Count of Mortain	Hanging Houghton	2h − 1v	4¾h	4p
Walter the Fleming	Hanging Houghton	2v + 1 bov		—
Countess Judith	Hanging Houghton	1h + 1v		2p
Bury St Edmunds Abbey	Lamport	1v + 1 bov		1p
Countess Judith	Lamport	1 bov	4¾h	—
Walter the Fleming	Lamport	4h + 1v		2p
Bury St Edmunds Abbey	Scaldwell	1h + 3v		3p
Countess Judith	Scaldwell	2h + 1v	4¾h	4p
Bishop of Coutances	Scaldwell	3v		1p
Countess Judith	Walgrave	3h + 3v		7p
Count of Mortain	Walgrave	½h	9h + ½v	2p
King	Walgrave & Old	2h + 3½v		7p
King	Faxton	2h		12p
	Totals	32h + 105a		83p

XVI Orlingbury

Domesday Tenant-in-Chief	*Holding*	*Hides*		*Ploughlands*
King	Cransley	2h + 1v		(4p)*
Guy de Reinbuedcurt	Cransley	1½h	4¾h	3p
Countess Judith	Cransley	1h		—
Bishop of Coutances	Broughton	2h + 3v		5p
Countess Judith	Broughton	1½h	4¾h	3p
King	Broughton	½h		(1p)*
Peterborough Knights	Pytchley	1½h†		—
William Engaine	Pytchley	2h	9½h	4p
Count of Mortain	Pytchley	3v		1½p
Peterborough Knights	Pytchley	5h + 1v†		13p
Bishop of Coutances	Isham	3v		1p
Guy de Reinbuedcurt	Isham	1h + 2½v	4¾h	3p
Eustace	Isham	1h + 2½v		3p
Count of Mortain	Orlingbury	3v		1½p
Bishop of Coutances	Harrowden	2h + 3v		6p
Guy de Reinbuedcurt	Harrowden	1h	4¾h	2p
Countess Judith	Hardwick	1h		2p
King	Part of Finedon	3h + 1v	4¾h	(6p)‡
Bishop of Coutances	Harrowden	1½h		3p
Bishop of Coutances	Harrowden	1h + 1v		2p
Count of Mortain	Hannington	½h } 1h + 1v	5h	1p
Countess Judith	Hannington	3v }		—
Walter the Fleming	Withmale in Orlingbury	2h + 2v		2p
	Totals	38h + 30a		67p

* Rated together at 5p.

† These two holdings are shown by the Northants. Survey to be independent estates.

‡ Estimated share of total ploughlands.

XVII South *Navereslund*

Domesday Tenant-in-Chief	*Holding*	*Hides*		*Ploughlands*	
King	Finedon	9½h	10h	(19½p)*	
Bishop of Coutances	Finedon	½h		2p	
Peterborough Abbey	Irthlingborough	5h + 1v	10h	15p	
Peterborough Knights	Irthlingborough	5h − 1v		—	
Peterborough Knights	Woodford	7h	10h	12p	
Peterborough Knights	Little Addington	3h		8p	
Bishop of Coutances	Little Addington	1h + 1v	2½h	3p	
Bishop of Coutances	Woodford	1h + 1v		2p	
Peterborough Knights	Woodford	3v		—	
Bishop of Coutances	Great Addington	1½h		2p	6p
Crowland Abbey	Great Addington	2h		4p	
	Totals	36h + 3v		67½p	

XVIII North *Navereslund*

Domesday Tenant-in-Chief	*Holding*	*Hides*			*Ploughlands*	
Peterborough Abbey	Kettering	10h			16p	
Guy de Reinbuedcurt	Burton Latimer	8½h		10h	14p	
Bishop of Coutances	Burton Latimer	1½h			3p	
Robert Albus	Grafton Underwood	3h	3½h	10h	8p	9p
Eustace	Grafton Underwood	½h			1p	
Bury St Edmunds Abbey	Warkston	3½h			9p	
Peterborough Knights	Cranford	3h			6p	
Peterborough Knights	Cranford	1½h			3p	
Bishop of Coutances	Cranford	1v			1p	
Bishop of Coutances	Barton Seagrave	4½h			10p	
	Totals	36h + 1v			71p	

* Estimated share of total ploughlands allotted in DB to the Finedon complex.

XIX Rothwell

Domesday Tenant-in-Chief	*Holding*	*Hides*			*Ploughlands*	
St Mary of Grestain	Braybrook	2h	$\frac{10h}{3}$		4p	
Robert de Veci	Braybrook	1h			2p	
Robert de Buci	Braybrook	$\frac{1}{3}$h			$\frac{1}{2}$p	
Countess Judith	Braybrook	$\frac{1}{2}$v	$\frac{6h}{3}$	$\frac{20h}{3}$	—	
Bury St Edmunds Abbey	Braybrook	$\frac{1}{2}$v			$\frac{1}{2}$p	
Robert de Buci	Braybrook	$\frac{1}{2}$h			1p	
Countess Judith	Braybrook	1h + 1v			2p	
Count of Mortain	Desborough	1v	$\frac{6h}{3}$		1p	6p
Robert de Todeni	Desborough	$\frac{1}{2}$h			2p	
William Peverell	Desborough	1h + 1v			3p	
Bury St Edmunds Abbey	Arthingworth	$\frac{1}{2}$v	$\frac{8h}{3}$		—	
King	Arthingworth	$\frac{1}{2}$v			(–)*	
Count of Mortain	Arthingworth	2h + 1$\frac{2}{3}$v			5p	
Count of Mortain	Thorpe Malsor	1$\frac{1}{3}$h	$\frac{30h}{3}$		3p	
King	Rothwell & Orton	8$\frac{2}{3}$h			40p	
King	Loddington	1$\frac{1}{3}$h	$\frac{20h}{3}$		(–)*	
St Mary of Grestain	Harrington	5h + $\frac{1}{3}$h			10p	
St Mary of Grestain	Newbottle Bridge in Harrington	$\frac{2}{3}$h	$\frac{5h}{3}$		1$\frac{1}{2}$p	
William Peverell	Kelmarsh†	1v			—	
King	Part of Finedon	$\frac{3}{4}$h			($\frac{1}{2}$p)	
King	Draughton	1h + $\frac{1}{2}$v	$\frac{5h+1v}{3}$		(–)*	
Countess Judith	Draughton	2$\frac{1}{2}$v			—	
King	Glendon	$\frac{1}{2}$h + $\frac{1}{3}$h	$\frac{5h}{3}$		(–)*	
St Mary of Grestain	Glendon	$\frac{1}{2}$h + $\frac{1}{3}$h			2p	
Walter the Fleming	Pipewell in Wilbarston	$\frac{1}{2}$h	$\frac{4h}{3}$		1p	4p
Robert de Todeni	Pipewell in Wilbarston	$\frac{1}{2}$h			2p	
Count of Mortain	Pipewell in Wilbarston	$\frac{1}{3}$h			1p	
Robert de Todeni	Rushton	1$\frac{1}{2}$h	$\frac{13h}{3}$		4p	
Countess Judith	Rushton	2$\frac{1}{2}$h + $\frac{1}{3}$h			5p	
St Mary of Grestain	Rushton	$\frac{1}{2}$v	$\frac{3v}{3}$		$\frac{1}{2}$p	
King	Desborough	$\frac{1}{2}$v			(–)*	
	Totals	37$\frac{2}{3}$h (= $\frac{131}{3}$h)			98$\frac{1}{2}$p	

* These five holdings were rated at 7p. † Gelds in Arthingworth.

XX *Stotfalde*

Domesday Tenant-in-Chief	*Holding*	*Hides*			*Ploughlands*
Count of Mortain	Haselbeech		3h		9p
Bury St Edmunds Abbey	Maidwell	$\frac{1}{3}$v		$\frac{27}{3}$h	—
Ansger the Chaplain	Maidwell	1h + 3v	6h		—
Manno	Maidwell	4h + $\frac{2}{3}$v			8p
King	Kelmarsh	2h + $\frac{1}{3}$v	$3\frac{1}{2}$h + $\frac{2}{3}$v = $\frac{11}{3}$h		(4p)*
William Peverell	Kelmarsh	$1\frac{1}{2}$h + $\frac{1}{3}$v			4p
Countess Judith	Oxendon	1h		$\frac{21}{3}$h	2p
Count of Mortain	Oxendon	1h + $\frac{1}{3}$v	3h + $1\frac{1}{3}$v = $\frac{10}{3}$h		2p
King	Oxendon	1h + 1v			(2p)*
Count of Mortain	Little Bowden		2h + $1\frac{1}{3}$v = $\frac{7}{3}$h		6p
Bury St Edmunds Abbey	East Farndon	$\frac{1}{2}$h + $\frac{1}{3}$v			1p
Count of Mortain	East Farndon	$3\frac{1}{3}$v	2h + $1\frac{1}{3}$v = $\frac{7}{3}$h	$\frac{21}{3}$h	2p
Countess Judith	East Farndon	1v			$\frac{1}{4}$p
William	East Farndon	3v + $\frac{1}{3}$v			1p
Hugh de Grenmaisnil	Marston Trussel & Thorpe Lubenham		2h + $1\frac{1}{3}$v = $\frac{7}{3}$h		$4\frac{1}{2}$p
Bury St Edmunds Abbey	Clipston	$2\frac{1}{2}$v	1h		1p
King	Clipston	$1\frac{1}{2}$v			(1p)*
Bishop of Coutances	Clipston	$1\frac{2}{3}$v	$\frac{1}{2}$h		—
William Lovet	*unnamed*	$\frac{1}{3}$v		$\frac{28}{3}$h	—
Count of Mortain	Sibertoft		3h − 1v		9p
Geoffrey de Wirce	Sulby	$2\frac{1}{2}$h	5h + $\frac{1}{3}$v		5p
Guy de Reinbuedcurt	Sulby	$2\frac{1}{2}$h + $\frac{1}{3}$v			—
Bishop of Coutances	Clipston	$\frac{1}{2}$h + $\frac{3}{4}$v			3p
Bury St Edmunds Abbey	Comb in Clipston	$\frac{1}{2}$h	2h + $\frac{1}{4}$v	$\frac{6h + \frac{3}{4}v}{3}$	$\frac{1}{2}$p
Bury St Edmunds Abbey	Hothorpe	$3\frac{1}{2}$v			1p
	Totals	$34\frac{1}{3}$h + $\frac{1}{4}$v = $\frac{103h + \frac{3}{4}v}{3}$			$66\frac{1}{4}$p

* These three estates of the king were assessed together at 7p.

XXI *Stoche*

Domesday Tenant-in-Chief	*Holding*	*Hides*			*Ploughlands*	
King	Rockingham	1h	8h		3p	17p
Peterborough Abbey	Cottingham	7h			14p	
Count of Mortain	Carlton	3v			3p	
Ralph Pagenel	*unnamed**	2h	$3\frac{5}{12}$h		4p	8p
Robert de Buci	Ashley	$\frac{2}{3}$h			1p	
Robert de Buci	Ashley	$\frac{1}{3}$h			$\frac{1}{2}$p	
Countess Judith	Ashley	$\frac{1}{3}$h			(–)†	
Robert de Todeni	Ashley	$\frac{1}{3}$h	4h		1p	$7\frac{1}{2}$p+
Robert de Todeni	Ashley	3h			6p	
Robert de Todeni	Wilbarston	3h + 1v	4h		6p	8p
King	Wilbarston	3v			2p	
King	Stoke Albany	1h	4h		2p	8p
Robert de Todeni	Stoke Albany	3h			6p	
Robert de Buci	Weston by Welland	2h + $\frac{2}{3}$h	4h		6p	6p+
Countess Judith	Weston by Welland	1h + $\frac{1}{3}$h			(–)†	
Countess Judith	Sutton Bassett	$\frac{1}{2}$h + ($\frac{1}{3} \times \frac{1}{2}$)h	2h		(–)†	
Robert de Buci	Sutton Basset	1h + ($\frac{2}{3} \times \frac{1}{2}$)h		4h	$2\frac{1}{2}$p	$3\frac{1}{2}$p +
Robert de Buci	Brampton Ash	1h	2h		1p	
Countess Judith	Brampton Ash	1h			(–)†	
Robert de Buci	Brampton Ash	2h	4h		4p	9p
Robert de Todeni	Brampton Ash	2h			5p	
Count of Mortain	Dingley	$1\frac{1}{3}$h + $1\frac{1}{2}$ bov	$2\frac{1}{3}$h		3p	
Robert de Todeni	Dingley	1h – $1\frac{1}{2}$ bov		$4\frac{5}{18}$h	2p	9p+
Robert de Buci	Dingley	$\frac{2}{3}$h + ($\frac{2}{3} \times \frac{2}{3}$)h	2h – $\frac{1}{18}$h		4p	
Countess Judith	Dingley	$\frac{1}{3}$h + ($\frac{3}{4} \times \frac{2}{3}$)h			(–)†	
	Totals	39h + 83a			$80\frac{1}{2}$p	

* Probably in Carlton—see J. H. Round, *VCH, Northants.*, I, p. 386, n. 2.

† Part of 8p in *Hwicceslea*—approximate total share = $4\frac{1}{2}$p.

XXII Corby

Domesday Tenant-in-Chief	*Holding*	*Hides*				*Ploughlands*	
King	Weekley	2½h				6p	
Westminster Abbey	Boughton House in Weekley	1h			5h	2p	
Gunfrid de Cioches	Boughton House in Weekley	½h	2½h			1p	
Bury St Edmunds Abbey	Boughton House in Weekley*	1h				2p	
Gunfrid de Cioches	Newton	3v + 1 bov + ⅓ bov				2p	
Countess Judith	Newton	3v + 1 bov + ⅓ bov	2h + 3v			2p	6p
Countess Judith	Newton	3v + 1 bov + ⅓ bov			5h	2p	
Bury St Edmunds Abbey	Geddington	1h + 1v	2h + 1v			2p	
King	Geddington	1h				(3p)†	
Robert de Buci	Great Weldon	1h + 3v				5p	
Robert de Buci	Great Weldon	1v	2½h			—	8p
Hugh Ivry	Little Weldon	½h			5h	3p	
Westminster Abbey	Deene	2½h				8p	
King	Corby	1½h	5h			9p	
King	Brigstock	3½h				9p	
King	Gretton	3h + 3v				14p	16p
Richard	Kirby Hall in Gretton	1v	5h			2p	
King	land in "Geritone" hundred	1h				(2p)	
Countess Judith	Harringworth	5h				16p	
Eudo son of Hubert	Wakerley	2½h				6p	
William	Laxton	1½h				4p	
Robert de Buci	Blatherwick	2h	5h + ½v			6p	
Countess Judith	Oakley	1½h + ½v			10h + ½v	5p	
Bishop of Coutances	Stanion	1½v	3v			2p	
King	Stanion	1½v		2½h		(1p)†	
King	Islip (member of Brigstock)	1h + 3v				(4p)†	
	Totals	40h + 15ac				118p	

* Rubricated in DB under Rothwell, erroneously.

† Assessed together as 8p.

XXIII Huxloe*

Domesday Tenant-in-Chief	*Holding*	*Hides*			*Ploughlands*
Guy de Reinbuedcurt	Cranford	3v			3p
Peterborough Abbey	Slipton	1h + 1v		5h	2p
Bishop of Coutances	Islip	1h + 1v			2p
Bishop of Coutances	Lowick	2h − 1v			3p
King	Barnwell all Saints	6h + 1v			6p
Richard	Benefield	3v		10h	2p
Westminster Abbey	Sudborough	3h			8p
Ramsey Abbey	Barnwell St Andrew	6h			8p
Countess Judith	Twywell	1½h	3h		2p
King	Part of Finedon	1½h			(2½p)†
Thorney Abbey	Twywell	3h − 1½v		15h	3p
Sibold	Lowick	1½v	3h		7p
Peterborough Knights	Aldwinckle St Peters	3h			1½p
Guy de Reinbuedcurt	Aldwinckle All Saints	5h		10h	9p
Countess Judith	Lilford	5h			14p
	Totals	40h			73p

* It is also possible to arrange the holdings in this hundred in 3h units.

† Estimated ploughland assessment for this part of Finedon.

XXIV Navisford

Domesday Tenant-in-Chief	*Holding*	*Hides*			*Ploughlands*	
Peterborough Abbey	Stoke Doyle	2h + 1v	5h		8p	
Peterborough Knights	Stoke Doyle	2h + 3v			—	
Bishop of Coutances	Wadenhoe	2h + ½v	2½h	5h	6p	
Peterborough Knights	Wadenhoe	1½v			—	
Peterborough Knights	Pilton	2½h			5p	
Bishop of Coutances	Wadenhoe	2½h + 1 bov	9½h + 1 bov		5p	
Peterborough Knights	Thorpe Achurch	6½h			10p	
Peterborough Abbey	Clapton	½h			1p	8p
Peterborough Knights	Clapton	3h + 3v	5h		5p	
Eustace	Clapton	1h + 1v			2p	
Oger	Thrapston	2½h	3h + 1v	8h	5p	
Bishop of Coutances	Thrapston	3v			2p	
Peterborough Knights	Titchmarsh	3h + 1v			5p	
Peterborough Knights	Catworth	1½h			3p	
Henry de Ferriers	Titchmarsh	10h + ($\frac{2}{3} \times \frac{1}{2}$)h − 1v			15p	
	Totals	42h + 85a			72p	

XXV Polebrook

Domesday Tenant-in-Chief	*Holding*	*Hides*		*Ploughlands*	
Peterborough Knights	Armston & Kingsthorpe Lodge	5h		8p	
Peterborough Knights	Hemington	2½h	5h	4p	8p
Ramsey Abbey	Hemington	2½h		4p	
Peterborough Knights	Polebrook	4h − 1v	5h	8p	
Eustace	Polebrook	1h + 1v		2p	
Peterborough Knights	Winwick	½h		—	
Peterborough Abbey	Thurning	½h	2½h	½p	
Peterborough Knights	Luddington	1½h		3p	
Peterborough Abbey	Ashton	4½h		8p	
Peterborough Abbey	Oundle	6h	12½h	9p	
Crowland Abbey	Elmington Lodge	2h		3p	
Peterborough Abbey	Warmington	7½h		16p	
Peterborough Knights	Warmington	1½h	10h	—	
Crowland Abbey	Elmington Lodge	1h		1p	
Eustace	Winwick	½h		2p	
	Totals	40½h		68½p	

XXVI Willybrook

Domesday Tenant-in-Chief	*Holding*	*Hides*			*Ploughlands*	
Peterborough Knights	Lutton	2½h	3h		6p	
Ramsey Abbey	Lutton	½h			½p	
King	Tansor	6h			16p	
Peterborough Knights	Cotterstock	3h			6p	
Countess Judith	Fotheringhay	6h			12p	
Eustace	Woodnewton	3h			5p	
King	Nassington	6h			16p	
Peterborough Abbey	Elton	1½h	2h	3h	3p	
Ramsey Abbey	Elton	½h			½p	
Peterborough Knights	Warmington	1h			2p	
Eudo son of Hubert	Easton-on-the-Hill	1½h	2h	6h	4p	6p
Gilbert de Gand	Easton-on-the-Hill	½h			2p	
King	Kings Cliff	1h + 2½v	2h		14p	
Ramsey Abbey	Halefield Lodge in Apethorp	1½v			1p	
King	Apethorp	2h			12p	
King	Duddington	1h	3h		8p	
Ralph de Limesi	Colleyweston	2h			6p	
	Totals	39h			114p	

XXVII Nassaburgh (*Optonegrene*) (2 hundreds)

Domesday Tenant-in-Chief	*Holding*	*Hides*		*Ploughlands*	
Peterborough Abbey	Peterborough	8h	12h	16p	
Peterborough Abbey	Longthorpe	2h		4p	
Peterborough Knights	Milton	2h		3p	
Peterborough Knights	Werrington	3h		—	
Peterborough Abbey	Glinton	3h		30p	
Peterborough Abbey	Werrington	8¼h		30p	
Peterborough Knights	Glinton	10¼h		—	
Peterborough Abbey	Pilsgate	6h		6p	
William son of Ansculf	Barnack	3h		5p	
Peterborough Knights	Burghley (in St Martin's Without)	3v		2p	
Countess Judith	Wothorpe (= *Widethorp*)	3v	3h	1p	3p
Peterborough Knights	Wothorpe	3v		—	
Crowland Abbey	Wothorpe	1½h		2p	
Eudo son of Hubert	Easton-on-the-Hill	1½h		2p	
Peterborough Knights	Wittering	9h		16p	
Peterborough Knights	Southorpe	4½h		6p	
Peterborough Knights	Ailsworth	3h		—	
Peterborough Abbey	Ailsworth	6h		12p	
Peterborough Abbey	Castor	3h		12p	
Peterborough Knights	Castor	3h		—	
Richard Engaine	Stibbington	2h		2p	
	Totals	81h + 1v		149p	

XXVIII East *Hwicceslea*

Domesday Tenant-in-Chief	*Holding*	*Hides*	*Ploughlands*		
King	Ketton	7h	13p	21p	
King	Tixover	2h	8p		
Gilbert de Gand	Empingham	7½h + 1 bov	15p	21p	
Countess Judith	Tickencote	3h − 1 bov	6p		
William Peverell	Empingham	2½h	4p	14p	28p
Gilbert de Gand	Empingham	4h	8p		
Countess Judith	Horne	1h	2p		
Bishop of Durham	Horne	2h	4p	14p	
William son of Ansculf	Tolthorpe	½h	4p		
Bishop of Lincoln	Essendine	1h	6p		
David	Little Casterton	3v	1½p	10½p	21p
King	Great Casterton	3½h	9p		
Countess Judith	Ryhall	1½h } 3h	2½p*	10½p	
	Belmesthorpe	1½h			
Peterborough Abbey	Tinewell	5h + 1v	8p		
	Totals	43h	91p		

* Ryhall was assessed at 8p, but this included appendages of Ryhall at Belmesthorpe, Ashley, Sutton Bassett, Weston by Welland, Dingley, and Brampton (*VCH*, *Northants.*, 1, pp. 350 a–b). The total hidage of the estate was 7⅙h, so that 2½p is a not unreasonable estimate of the number of ploughlands for which Ryhall and Belmesthorpe (each 1½-hide holdings) were assessed.

XXIX West *Hwicceslea*

Domesday Tenant-in-Chief	*Holding*	*Hides*		*Ploughlands*		
Robert de Todeni	Barrowden	1v	4h	—	28p	
King	Barrowden	4h − 1v		10p		
King	Morcot	4h		8p		
King	North Luffenham	4h		10p		
King	Seaton	1½h + 1 bov		6p	14p	28p
King	Thorpe-by-Water	1h + 1v		4p		
King	Bisbrook & Glaston	1½h		4p		
King	South Luffenham, Kelthorpe	7h + 1v		14p		
Countess Judith	Glaston	4h		8p	28p	
Robert de Todeni	Seaton	1h + 1 bov		4p		
Bishop of Lincoln	Liddington, Dry Stoke, *Snelsdon*, Caldecote	2h		16p		
Countess Judith	Bisbrook	2h + 1v		3½p		
	Totals	33h		87½p		

26/10?

OCCASIONAL PAPERS

FIRST SERIES

No. 1 H. P. R. Finberg *The Local Historian and his Theme* 3s. 6d. net

2 H. P. R. Finberg *The Early Charters of Devon and Cornwall* 10s. 6d. net

3 Joan Thirsk *Fenland Farming in the Sixteenth Century*
with an introduction by R. H. Tawney 10s. 6d. net

5 G. H. Martin *The Early Court Rolls of the Borough of Ipswich* 10s. 6d. net

7 C. F. Slade *The Leicestershire Survey (c. A.D. 1130)*
with a preface by Sir Frank M. Stenton 16s. net

8 H. P. R. Finberg *Roman and Saxon Withington: a Study in Continuity* 10s. 6d. net

10 Cyril Hart *The Early Charters of Essex: the Saxon Period* 10s. 6d. net

11 Cyril Hart *The Early Charters of Essex: the Norman Period* 10s. 6d. net

13 W. G. Hoskins *The Westward Expansion of Wessex*
with a supplement to No. 2 in this series, by H. P. R. Finberg 12s. net

14 Thomas Garden Barnes *The Clerk of the Peace in Caroline Somerset* 10s. 6d. net

15 R. B. Smith *Blackburnshire: a Study in Early Lancashire History* 10s. 6d. net

16 L. A. Burgess *The Origins of Southampton* 10s. 6d. net

17 K. J. Allison, M. W. Beresford, and J. G. Hurst, *et al.*
The Deserted Villages of Oxfordshire 10s. 6d. net

18 K. J. Allison, M. W. Beresford, and J. G. Hurst, *et al.*
The Deserted Villages of Northamptonshire 10s. 6d. net

19 John S. Moore *Laughton: a Study in the Evolution of the Wealden Landscape* 12s. 6d. net

20 Margaret Spufford *A Cambridgeshire Community: Chippenham from Settlement to Enclosure*
12s. 6d. net

Numbers 4, 6, 9, and 12 are out of print

SECOND SERIES

No. 1 Alan Everitt *Change in the Provinces: the Seventeenth Century* 15s. net

2 R. A. McKinley *Norfolk Surnames in the Sixteenth Century* 15s. net

3 Cyril Hart *The Hidation of Northamptonshire* 15s. net

In preparation

Michael Laithwaite *Urban House-Types*

C. V. Phythian-Adams *Coventry in Crisis, 1518–1525*

Philip Styles *Worcester Cathedral and the Dean and Chapter in the Seventeenth Century*

Alan Everitt *The Wealth of Northampton, 1570–1770*

Price 15s. net £0.75